PRAISE FOR *UNSILENCING THE 81%*

"From time to time we need to be reminded that government doesn't create and government doesn't innovate. They destroy, and they waste. John Rust does a good job of showing us the reality of how we have lost the idea that politicians and office holders are there to serve the people with delegated authority. They were never intended to be power brokers that can't be held accountable. It's time to get back to the basics. This book should help."

—Chad Prather

———

"Food. Quality, abundant, affordable food. The farming families of America are the lifeblood of life itself and John Rust in his book *Unsilencing the 81%*, celebrates the ongoing culture war on behalf of the American farming way of life. Without the unshackling of the American farmer, there is no American Dream."

—Ted Nugent

UNSILENCING THE 81%

8/1/24

UNSILENCING THE 81%

How one farmer is fighting
for conservative voices,
businesses, and families
in Indiana and beyond

JOHN RUST

MEDIA.COM

Published by
Illumify Media Global
www.IllumifyMedia.com
"Let's bring your book to life!"

Library of Congress Control Number: 2024902615

Paperback ISBN: 978-1-959099-75-8
Hardcover ISBN: 978-1-959099-76-5

Cover design by Debbie Lewis

Printed in the United States of America

CONTENTS

FOREWORD

GET READY TO BE inspired by a story of hard work and the American Dream! I'm thrilled to introduce y'all to John Rust, a true American original and a patriotic farmer who doesn't just raise hens but is also raising the bar for freedom-loving folks everywhere.

In this exciting journey through time and the heartland of our nation, John lays out what it means to be a patriot and a farmer, and what the American Dream is all about. Like so many of us, his story began generations ago and his goal is to protect America so others can create stories like his for generations to come. Being an eighth-generation rancher myself, I appreciate his obvious work ethic and commitment to getting things done, no matter what obstacles he has to overcome.

During my decades in agriculture, I've seen my fair share of hardworking folks, but John stands out. His dedication to the principles that make our nation great—freedom, self-reliance, tenacity, and a healthy dose of farmer's grit—shines through this book about his life and an America that he intends to serve and protect.

This isn't your run-of-the-mill farm tale; it's a no-nonsense, common-sense testimonial for those who believe in the power of free markets, opportunity, and good old American prosperity. John's life has been packed with examples of why our nation is the world's best example of freedom and opportunity. Unfortunately, it's also been packed with examples of just how fragile those things are, and how eager powerful people are to restrict them.

Every page and every story take you on a wild ride that exposes the challenges, dangers, and frustrations faced by American farmers and all our hardworking citizens. As we farmers do, he says it like it is and shows he's not afraid to tackle an issue head-on. But this book isn't just about farming; it's a cautionary tale and a call to protect our nation from government corruption and the creeping authoritarianism, as John exposes how very real this danger is to us all, even if we don't yet see it.

Whether you're a seasoned farmer, a patriot, or just someone who enjoys a good read about hard work, liberty, and American opportunity, *Unsilencing the 81%* will captivate and inspire you.

God bless John, God bless our farmers, and God bless the land of the free.

—Sid Miller
Texas Commissioner of Agriculture

INTRODUCTION

OUR GOVERNMENT IS FULL of bad eggs that are years past their "freshness date," and unless someone steps up and makes a change, the American Dream will no longer be an American Reality.

Intended to serve the people, our government is riddled with politicians who partner with powerful cronies to cheat the hardworking citizens, the backbone of this great nation, out of success and prosperity. Instead of serving us, they serve themselves at our expense. Mountains of regulations cripple innovation and opportunity as a ploy to control what was meant to be free—the market and the people. Those of us with the work ethic to achieve success are brought to heel by individuals and organizations who see our success as a threat to their power.

American greatness was built by the little guy, but we are the ones who shoulder the brunt of the burden caused by government incompetence, irresponsibility, and deflected blame. They do what's convenient—not what's right—no matter who is harmed along the way, perpetually kicking the can down the road for someone else to deal with. As a result, our economy has been decimated and our society is more divided than it has ever been.

Imagine instead an America where dedication and work ethic are fostered and rewarded rather than stunted by lazy and conniving career politicians who prefer to ride the gravy train into a taxpayer-funded retirement. Imagine a free market where excellence and ingenuity determine who rises to the top, not powerful corporations or politicians leveraging laws and regulations to eliminate competition.

Imagine an America where our politicians represent citizens with integrity and commitment rather than playing a carefully crafted political game, the rules to which you aren't allowed to know. In a government for and by the people, citizens should never be treated as mere pawns in a competition of wealth and power. And yet, that's exactly what has happened, and it needs to be stopped.

Growing up on a rural midwestern egg farm, I was surrounded by examples of integrity, commitment, and hard work, values which became deeply entrenched in my own character. I was part of an endeavor that embodied the American Dream—a small business that started from nothing but a young man's idea and a pickup truck, and grew into a company that now serves hundreds of millions of our local and global neighbors.

I learned very young to value freedom, independence, determination, and perseverance. I worked hard to earn everything I had and appreciated my success all the more for it, even if I didn't always enjoy the struggles along the way.

As a farmer, I was always up at the crack of dawn, ready to put in a full day's work caring for our chickens and keeping our family's egg farm running. I was an integral part of a team that cared not only for our hens, but also for those who worked for our company and the many consumers who depended on us. My father didn't just show me how to run a chicken farm; he taught me how to think critically, show compassion, serve others, and defend what is right.

I endured attacks by Mother Nature, violent radical activists, mega-corporations, and even the government, all of whom sought to control or destroy me. But they've never won.

Instead of submitting, I stand and fight, no matter the opponent. Be it a blizzard or a lawsuit, these battles have only strengthened my resolve to do what is right and stand up for the little guy.

My most recent battle is still ongoing as of 2024, and surely my most important yet—a battle for the rights and freedoms of my fellow Hoosiers.

Despite facing powerful and controlling entities my entire life, I never realized the magnitude of the threat against the American people until I decided to step up and face it head on. I wanted to be part of the change needed in our struggling nation, but powerful and controlling forces within our own government sought to prevent me from doing so.

The political establishment uses cunning and trickery to hand-select candidates and concentrate power with those who are willing to play their corrupt game. Unsuspecting voters are presented a mere illusion of choice and citizens are swindled out of their rights and freedoms. In fact, 81% of Hoosiers were unknowingly and craftily eliminated from eligibility to run for office, paving the way for decades of corrupt career politicians. That is, until I stepped into the fray.

I've never been one to shy away from a fight for justice, and this time was no different. I knew what I would have to do.

I will fight for that unsuspecting 81%. I will fight for the hardworking Americans who are languishing under the weight of powerful entities that are destroying the values and principles that make the American Dream possible.

I will fight to restore decency to America, and to prevent radical activism and ideological indoctrination from permeating every facet of American society and government. I will fight to ensure that the interests of hardworking Americans are being served, not those of special interest groups, mega-corporations, or an increasingly authoritarian government.

I will fight—not for myself, but for you—to bring the integrity, work ethic, and commitment of an American farmer to Washington. This is a story of how I went from gathering eggs to fighting for the future of America. Hopefully, it is but the prologue to a story about our fight to make America decent and prosperous again.

1

HATCHING THE
AMERICAN DREAM

GROWING UP WITH AN incredibly tenacious and stubborn father meant days filled with sweat, sometimes tears, and a whole lot of life lessons. Once Dad set his mind to something, we knew it was going to get done. While that sometimes rubs people the wrong way, it taught me valuable lessons about dedication, commitment, follow-through, and creating success. In fact, dedication to a single simple product would ultimately shape the course of my life and grow me into the man I am today.

That product was eggs.

Back in the early 1930s, my dad's parents built two chicken houses. These weren't your ordinary little household coops; these hen houses were designed to hold 500 chickens each, providing around 800 eggs daily, as chickens lay about 5 eggs a week.

Personally, I love eggs! I can scarf down a plate of eggs anytime, any way—boiled, scrambled, over easy, sunny side up, and especially deviled. I always love the ones brought to my local church and community events by Olga Otte, the organist at Borchers. She regularly brings dozens of deviled eggs to activities, and they are gulped down quickly by all!

But I wasn't in the picture yet, and 800 eggs was certainly more than the Rust household could enjoy alone. They were meant to be sold to provide essential income for a family farm.

1

It was my dad, David Rust, who hatched a business plan to sell the eggs. He had honed his sales skills beforehand raising money to benefit his community. Over the summers of 1947 and '48, Dad got together with Harlan Dringenburg and other members of the Luther League of young men, or "Borchers" to the community, named after the first preacher of the local St. Paul Lutheran church. Working tirelessly through those summer months, these young men raised $4,700 selling freshly picked sweet corn at the Indianapolis Municipal Market, then located near the parking lot of the present-day Eli Lilly and Company building near downtown Indianapolis.

With that $4,700 dollars, the group of young men purchased a beautiful new pipe organ for the church, the contract for which was signed by my great uncle Clarence Wente. Thanks to the entrepreneurial dedication of my father and the spirit of accomplishing good for the community within so many at our church, Harlan would go on to spend decades accompanying the church congregation as the organist. I spent many Sundays singing hymns along with that beautiful instrument, which would eventually be played at my father's funeral.

Shortly thereafter, the church upgraded to a new organ, and I brought home the original pipe organ Dad had helped buy so long ago. We set it up in my home, where I still play it to this day. Every time I sit down at this beautiful old instrument and play a hymn, I'm reminded of the legacy of hard work I carry on.

The next summer, Dad decided to keep going to Indianapolis, having found a successful market for Jackson County freshly picked sweet corn. While he was at it, he decided to sell eggs from the two hen houses as well, which had previously been sold to local firms that would pick up eggs from farms in the area.

Every day that the market was open, Dad was up at 3 a.m. to load sweet corn and eggs into the bed of his late '40s-model Chevy pickup truck and head off to the city to sell that day's produce. He had his truck painted up with a stylized "Dave's Produce," building himself a reputation in Indianapolis as a local produce distributor from Jackson County.

As business ramped up for Dave's Produce, his family's 1,000 hens quickly became but a drop in the bucket of how many eggs he needed. He started driving around to other local farms in the county to buy their eggs. This began decades of business growth and expansion centered on a single product—eggs.

Dave's Produce successfully operated out of the bed of that pickup for several years and while the sweet corn was an early part of the business, it was the farm fresh eggs that truly stole the show. Around 1950, something happened that would change the business—he didn't sell all his eggs at the farmer's market. Every day for years, he had happily come home with an empty truck bed and a pocket full of cash and coin. But not this day. The consistent business model that had served him so well had finally cracked.

But that didn't stop Dad. Instead of going home with unsold eggs, he considered this a new business opportunity and drove straight to a new grocery store on the south side of Indianapolis. While small by today's standards, this store was one of the first modern independent grocery stores in Indianapolis. Not only were they interested in buying Dad's farm-fresh eggs, but they even ordered more for the next week! This dedication to creating his own success rather than waiting for success to land in his lap would be instrumental in building a massive and essential nationwide business.

I've learned a lot of lessons from Dad that included the words, "but that didn't stop me!" I'm grateful that he instilled this work ethic in me as I've hit a heck of a lot of speed bumps along my own path. Instead of cracking, now I simply seek out another way to push forward.

When Dad came back to that grocery store with next week's order, the store owner had taken it upon himself to call two other nearby stores and suggest Dave's Produce as an egg supplier. Thus, a new door-to-door egg sales route was born, breaking the business away from the smaller scale farmer's market scene and quickly growing into the grocery store distribution scene. Supermarkets were just starting to pop up at this time and they were looking for suppliers who could handle these larger orders. Dad expanded quickly, adding more trucks and hiring drivers to help him deliver eggs to an expanded area all through Indianapolis and into surrounding cities as well.

During the next decade, Dad added many more stores to his routes. To meet the ever-increasing demands, he bought eggs from local family farms all over Jackson County, passing along the success to his neighbors. As business flourished, Dad saw that their own two hen houses and a handful of their neighbors' chicken coops wouldn't be enough. He needed to increase his production in a big way.

In 1955, Dad built the first of many larger chicken houses. At least, they were large for the time. Mom and Dad had just bought their own farm after getting married, and this new location became known as "Rose Acres," from what neighbors used to call Grandma and Grandpa Rust's original farm, which was fenced in by multiflora rose bushes.

This 'new' Rose Acres quickly supplanted the original in terms of the number of chickens. New hen houses were built for the rapidly expanding demand for eggs. The first

4

two were named "Texas" and "Tennessee," each with around 1,800 chickens. Then came "Kentucky," which was designed to hold 2,400 hens. Then came "Washington," "Alabama," "Alaska," and "Siberia," each with more chickens until they had over 100,000 chickens on the new Rose Acre Farms. This massive expansion of production capability put him on track to grow the business exponentially. His success was no longer dependent on farms with a potentially erratic supply, but on himself and his own hard work.

This is another important life lesson I learned from Dad— dependence on others limits our possibilities. One of the greatest things about America is that we all have the freedom to create our own success, as long as we're willing to work for it. I was taught that I have limitless possibilities for personal, educational, social, or business success, as long as I remain dedicated to my goals and am willing to follow through on what it takes to achieve them. My own work ethic is my only limiting factor. No one cares as much about my goals as I do, and no one is going to work as hard to achieve them as I will, which is why I strive to maintain independence in all aspects of my life.

By 1959, Dad had essentially captured a big portion of the Indianapolis grocery store egg market, and he had no intention of slowing down. In fact, he and Mom had their eye on other cities, and that year, he started his first sizable chicken farm to meet the anticipated demand. The structure was shaped like an octagon, but we called it Pentagon One, or P1 for short. It looked like quite a strange farm from above, with a large central building and long skinny "arms" branching off the sides. With seven chicken houses that could hold 10,000 birds each, the Pentagon One farm sustained 70,000 laying hens.

Pentagon 2 quickly followed. This farm was built for the needs of just one customer, A&P in Detroit and other nearby cities. The Atlantic and Pacific Tea Company had their own brand for eggs (Sunny Brook) and so the eggs produced at Pentagon 2 were the first that were sold without the "Rose Acre" brand.

The next 20 years would be spent growing a family and the business. In 1966, dad built a new style of egg farm, Look Acres, that could sustain 100,000 hens. Two years later, when that was no longer enough, he built Egg Acres with a 400,000-hen capacity. And just three years after that, he built his first megafarm in Jennings County. "Jen Acres" could house a whopping 1.2 million laying hens. This massive farm is where I spent much of my childhood.

Perhaps a hundred feet from the hen houses stood the white farmhouse where I grew up with my mother, father, four brothers, and two sisters. Life was full of sharing, whether it was the workload or personal space, including sharing a single bathroom. At times, it was a bit of a nightmare with 9 of us all clamoring for space. But we made it through together.

As a boy, I spent a lot of time in the hen houses, either fetching a few eggs for one of Mom's many recipes, or gathering thousands of eggs during snow storms when many folks couldn't make it in to work. As you can imagine, we ate a heck of a lot of eggs. Usually, Mom cooked them in the hot bacon grease after taking the bacon strips off the pan. If bacon wasn't on the menu, then the eggs were fried in butter. Either way, they were always delicious.

Mom is a fantastic cook and we never really got tired of the eggs or other recipes she made for us. In fact, I developed and tested all the recipes that were printed on our egg cartons back in the 1990s, including deviled eggs, French toast, and sugar cookies, to name a few. These days, I still eat a lot of eggs, but now I tend to go back and forth between over-easy and scrambled, unless Olga Otte's deviled eggs are an option.

Aside from fetching eggs for cooking, one of my main jobs growing up was to sweep up the seemingly endless aisles running between the chicken cages. It felt like an exercise in futility at the time because no matter how much dust and feathers I swept up in one day, they all seemed to be back the next. But I was expected to keep on top of the project, especially considering it was essential to the cleanliness of the facility and therefore the health of the chickens that were the foundation of our family's business.

From a young age, Mom and Dad taught the value of hard work along with the satisfaction of seeing success from all that effort. My siblings and I were held to a high standard and given the opportunity to be involved in every aspect of the business as our capabilities and maturity would allow. Through the decades, every member of the family has continued to be involved in the company, contributing their unique abilities to the success of the business. Growing ourselves and the business through dedication and hard work truly embodies the idea of a family business.

Along with hard work, one reason the business thrived was because of the large-scale production farms my dad was building, which gave our company an incredible cost advantage over the competition. We could sell the most eggs at a fair price for consumers and always use that money to grow the business and expand our egg production.

Each new farm Dad built was paid for by the profits of the previous farms. They were always paid off, so he owned his business and avoided debt. Just like in the early days of the business, when he took large scale production into his own hands by building a bigger chicken farm, this financial independence empowered him and prevented him from being beholden to others in both his personal life and in making decisions regarding the business. All the while, he was helping to make this nutritious and protein-packed food an incredible bargain for the American consumer.

The late 1970s was historic for both the company and the industry as my father built Cort Acres, named for the small town of Cortland, IN. With the capacity to house more than 3 million chickens, it became the single largest chicken farm in the world when it was built. It remained so for decades. This was also the first of our farms to face significant backlash. Some in the community were opposed to the construction of such a facility as they simply didn't want a massive chicken farm near their neighborhood.

Rose Acres faced public outrage, negative press, and even some legal fights in opposition to the farm. Ultimately, we were given permits to build the facility in this rural location. The fact of the matter is that agriculture has to exist somewhere, or no one gets their food. If grocery store shelves are going to be stocked with eggs, they must be produced, and that requires a facility in which they can be produced on a scale large enough to meet the public demand. Otherwise, consumers would have to raise their own chickens, which most people simply cannot do.

The massive increase in egg production ability at Cort Acres meant that in 1980, we were able to expand delivery to the east coast, and New York specifically. Almost all the eggs produced by Rose Acre Farms were delivered by our own drivers. In fact, quite a few of the drivers we had during this time are still with us today in a variety of capacities.

One man, Gary Bradley, was a truck driver for us in the early eighties, delivering eggs to the east coast mostly from Cort Acre and Jen Acre farms. He drove over four million miles delivering Rose Acres eggs to New York and other cities all over the Midwest. After many years, Gary underwent a heart transplant. While his new heart was an incredible gift, it came at a steep price. During the surgery, blood flow to his eyes was cut off and when he woke, he was blind. This ended his career as a truck driver, but Gary's experience was invaluable to the company.

We found him a spot at the front desk of our main corporate office where he takes calls all day, every day, not just dealing with typical office phone calls, but calls from drivers all around the country. He may not have his sight anymore, but he still knows the roads and how to drive them better than almost anyone. Gary frequently advises drivers who call in, talking them through tricky transportation situations. He is not just a long-time company employee, but a personal friend, advisor, and confidant.

That's how it is with many employees. They spend decades working, learning, and growing beside us. In a family-owned company, the employees aren't just ordinary workers; they become part of our extended family and lifelong friends. That's why I personally hate the term 'employee.' As I grew up working side-by-side with so many amazing people, that term never has seemed to fit. They have always simply been an integral part of my life and the fabric of what makes Rose Acres and similar businesses what they are. We prioritize each and every one, as they are the heart and soul of our operations.

After the construction of the massive Cort Acre farm in 1980, we continued expanding, adding a new 1.5 million capacity chicken farm almost every year from 1984-1989. First were farms in Newton County, White County, and Pulaski County, Indiana. Then we branched out to the birthplace of John Wayne and built Winterset Egg Farm in Winterset, Iowa, followed by Guthrie Center Egg Farm near Guthrie Center, Iowa.

In 1989, Dad retired from the company after making some decisions that threatened the stability of the business and risked the livelihoods of thousands of employees. While this was a difficult period for my family and me, enduring a measure of bad press and smear campaigns, we were determined to persevere, maintaining the integrity and success of the company for our customers, employees, and ourselves. My hardworking mother served as president of the company for many years, touching almost every aspect of the business and benevolently keeping everyone in line.

My second oldest brother, Marcus, was the Vice President of the company, and he had a vision for nationwide growth. Over the next two decades, we would either buy or build numerous facilities in several states. With Marcus' vision and leadership, and the constant efforts of my siblings and me, we ramped up our out-of-state expansion and were now selling eggs from coast to coast. We bought a farm in Lincoln County, Missouri that housed 800,000 hens, and then one near Knob Noster, Missouri near the Whiteman Air Force base in Johnson County, Missouri.

I spent decades traveling these states helping oversee these chicken farms, both during construction and upon completion to keep an eye on facility operations. If we were buying an existing facility, I would evaluate the property beforehand. I wasn't about to let the company buy a bad egg on my watch!

I remember one of my first visits to what would be our farm near Knob Noster, Missouri. I was used to the wide-open Midwestern skies, but I wasn't prepared for what I saw take flight. This time, it wasn't chickens, who really can't fly very far. This was another kind of bird up in the sky. The sleek black triangle of a B-2 stealth bomber cruised above me, departing from the nearby Air Force base. During the Gulf War, I remember seeing those powerful and stealthy birds return after completing their wartime missions. They served as a powerful reminder of the freedoms we enjoy in this great nation, and of all that has been sacrificed to make America a land of opportunity—opportunities like starting a business from the bed of a pickup truck.

To avoid having all our eggs in one basket, and after so much geographical expansion, we thought we'd take a crack at expanding our product options while still sticking with what we knew—eggs. In 1994, we bought a dry powdered egg white processing plant from Kraft Foods. Located in Marshall, Missouri, we called it the Marshall Drier Plant. This specific egg white product is used in a variety of fluffy and delicious recipes like angel food cake, meringue, and all your favorite name brand chocolate bars that have a "nougat" filling. After that, we bought a powdered egg company in Social Circle, Georgia called National Egg Products Company, or NEPCO for short. That facility came with a chicken farm near Madison, Georgia, and while we no longer operate the powdered egg plant, we still run the chicken farm.

We then built a farm in Stuart, Iowa, and purchased facilities in Oconee and Canon, Georgia, Germantown, Illinois, and Clinton County, Indiana. Then in the early 2000s, we built another massive chicken farm near Plymouth, NC. With room for 3.4 million hens, this facility was just slightly larger than Cort Acres.

This started a boom of change within the egg industry which took place during the 2000s and 2010s.

During this time, the family business faced one of its greatest hurdles to date. We caught wind that California was working to pass a law requiring that eggs sold in the state be from cage-free facilities. In anticipation, we started construction on a new chicken farm in Bouse, Arizona that would be an entirely cage-free facility. What seemed like a victory was short lived. California wasn't the only state with new regulations regarding cage space per chicken. Other states were quickly demanding only cage-free eggs.

In response to, or perhaps empowered by, public outcry regarding animal welfare, our egg customers required us to increase the cage space for each chicken in numerous states. These stipulations threatened to scramble our whole operation if we didn't act appropriately.

It is not feasible to rebuild all the existing cages to be larger. If the size of the cages were to remain the same, we would have to remove a chicken or two from each cage in order to comply with the new space requirements. If we did only this, these farms would have fewer chickens and therefore fewer eggs produced, leading to less revenue because of fewer eggs being sold.

Our main concern became the impact on our employees. As I said, they were basically extended family, and the last thing we wanted were layoffs. We knew that such a reduction of chickens at so many farms could also inadvertently lead to higher priced eggs, translating to a financial burden on our faithful customers, unless we found a solution.

Keep in mind, egg farming is a business with a very low return on equity over time—about 7% at most. We aren't in it for short term big bucks; we are in it for a long and steady business to be an integral part of the American food supply chain. And we certainly don't anticipate a lucky hen starting to lay golden eggs. We're egg farmers because it's in our blood and it's what we love.

What started as an opportunity to sell our own eggs and serve neighbors at the Indianapolis farmers market turned into a chance to supply eggs for breakfast plates on kitchen tables across the entire country. Our egg farms are no longer about making do; they're about providing a healthy food option for the people of this nation—people who can't do it themselves and people who count on us.

It was our duty to do right by those who depend on us and our eggs, and we made it our goal to overcome these potentially catastrophic regulations with the minimum amount of negative impact on both our beloved employees and customers.

It was my brother Marcus who hatched a bright idea to save the day, and after our customary family discussions on the subject, we had a plan. To put it simply, we added large chicken houses to many of our existing farms. This way we could remove chickens from cages to increase space, but not reduce the overall number of chickens producing eggs on those farms. This not only allowed us to comply with space requirements, but we were even able to increase production by adding the new houses and increasing our overall flock size.

We added two new chicken houses with hundreds of thousands of chickens apiece to the Johnson County, Guthrie Center, Lincoln County, and White County egg farms, and several additional houses to Pulaski County farm. Ultimately, we managed to increase our total bird numbers and therefore ramp up our total egg production. This helped increase the nation's egg supply instead of allowing these new regulations to curtail production, helping us keep both our customers and beloved employees satisfied.

Through all the trials, both large and small, the business has continued to blossom. In 2020, we began building another two million-hen capacity cage-free facility named Desert Valley in Arizona, and we are partners on a special project for a 400,000-capacity cage-free farm in Hawaii.

From 2002 to today, our total number of laying hens went from 15,300,000 to over 21,000,000. Adding these millions of new layers increased Rose Acres' ability to supply eggs to the nation even while we were increasing the space in the pens for the chickens by having fewer chickens per pen.

Though business success has provided ample opportunity to live anywhere in the country, I have always called Indiana home, staying close to family and home base. Until around 2006, all members of the family stayed close, working for the business in some capacity. Everyone had a role, everyone was consulted, and everyone's opinion was valued. Even still, many family members are instrumental in business operations and if there's ever an emergency of any kind, we all still chip in to help.

In 2012, we restructured the company and made Marcus the CEO with Mom the Chairman of the Board. As Mom has gotten older, she has remained incredibly sharp and hard-working, continuing to work 6:30-4:30 every day. At 89 years old, she's no spring chicken. But she watches the financial and production records like a hawk, as she has her entire life. And she still likes to visit farms when she can, to watch the company she helped build continue to grow and help feed America.

My brothers and sisters have all filled positions on boards, managed offices and technology, or worked the farms, always answering any all-hands-on-deck calls. My brother Anthony was in charge of monitoring the health and production of the flocks, as birds of different ages and breeds eat and lay differently, requiring careful observation and attention to keep them healthy. As the CEO, Marcus has always focused on business growth and expansion, prioritizing the construction of new chicken farms and increasing sales.

I was on the Board of Directors at an early age. While working my way through college at nearby Indiana University, I was chiefly dealing with helping the company transition from operating with my father at the helm to a family business not only guided by family, but also long-term, dedicated employees who work hard for Rose Acres to succeed.

During my time on the Board of Directors, I got to work closely with so many of my family members and touched so many different aspects of the company, from signing employee checks, approving purchase orders, dealing directly with customers, and making on-site visits to check out the farms. I even grabbed a broom every now and then to sweep an aisle that wasn't up to snuff.

I also kept my finger on the family pulse and acted as a sort of liaison within the family, some of whom weren't always eager to expand. Mixing business and family isn't always easy and many in a similar situation might find themselves resigned to walking on eggshells at home and the office. But we have always been committed to success and willing to put in the work to achieve it. I suspect we came by these character traits by both nature and nurture, as Dad isn't the only one who passed on tenacity and stubbornness. Just wait until you hear about my Grandma Otte.

2

THE PRINCIPLE OF THE THING

I'M HIGHLY DRIVEN TO achieve my goals and to fight hard for what's right, even if it's inconvenient. I developed this drive from seeing it first-hand in Mom and Dad, especially with starting a nationwide company from a truck bed. But I suspect some part of it runs in the blood and was genetically passed down to me by one of the most impressive women in the Midwest—Grandma Lura Otte.

While Rose Acres was busy expanding, Mom's mother, Lura Otte, had already made history, fundamentally changing the financial landscape of farming in rural middle America, especially for women. Her tenacious character carried her through a lawsuit not only to resolve an injustice she faced but to benefit hardworking women across the nation for years to come.

Sometimes you have to break a few eggs to make an omelet, and she was willing to make the necessary sacrifices to do the right thing.

Born in early January of 1911, Grandma Otte grew up on a farm, which is clearly a longstanding family tradition. She never finished high school because the family needed her working the farm. But that didn't stop her from being one of the most impressive women of her time.

She only graduated from the 8th grade, but was the top student academically in the county. Extremely well organized, self-motivated, and hardworking, she had a knack for finances and business. Apparently, she also had a knack for picking good eggs because in 1932, she married Everett Otte and they happily started their own farm.

Everett had an incredible work ethic, valued his independence, and had already proven he was committed to his goals by cutting timber and carefully saving until he had $7,000 to purchase a 109-acre farm with a single story farmhouse for himself and his new bride. Grandma and Grandpa were equal partners in marriage and farming, working the land and caring for the animals in tandem.

Farming back then, and even life in general, wasn't all it's cracked up to be. They faced immense challenges, notably the Great Depression and historically hostile weather. If it wasn't an extreme summer drought killing crops and animals, it was unusually frigid winters freezing almost every living thing. I don't know if I'd even be here if Grandma hadn't been determined enough to outlast these catastrophic hurdles and put in the immense work necessary to survive, much less thrive.

When Mother Nature tried to show Grandma who ruled the roost, she had a thing or two to say in response. Grandma was as powerful a force as any winter storm. Not only did she manage household duties and care for the animals, but she also tended to three gardens. She planted, harvested, and canned a variety of vegetables including green beans, peas, tomatoes, corn, grapes, peaches, and cherries.

Beyond tending her gardens, she worked the farm as much as almost anyone. Not only did she deliver food to Grandpa Otte in the fields, but she also often drove teams of animals herself, plowing or disking the fields, hauling hay, or delivering feed to town. She cared for livestock, milked cows, and helped with harvesting.

And if you thought she had a lot on her plate with all this, she also raised five kind, hardworking, and committed children who would go on to follow in her footsteps, positively contributing to society and raising families of their own.

On top of all this, she made it a point to serve in her community. She participated in numerous women's organizations, sang in the church choir, and played the organ for services. Grandma was a phenomenal pianist, and Mom told us many stories of the beautiful classical music she often played. While Mom insists her favorite was Beethoven's Moonlight Sonata, I wish I could have heard her popular and raucous version of Turkey in the Straw.

Mom also told us stories of how extremely precise and meticulous Grandma was. When I complained about being expected to stick to a chore schedule, Mom would tell me how Grandma kept a militant schedule around the house and the farm, and everyone knew what the plan was for each day—baking bread one day, washing clothes the next, ironing after that, and so on.

She also kept meticulous written records, a habit that would prove incredibly beneficial during a coming lawsuit that would be a landmark court case. My siblings and I grew up perpetually hounded to "write it down!" Mom learned this from Grandma Otte and claims it was essentially the motto for Grandma's life. She recorded almost every relevant metric you could think of including the weather, market prices for various products, crop yields, and acres of each crop. While my notes are mostly electronic and aren't about the weather, I seem to have also inherited the 'avid notetaker' gene, as I like to make sure things are written down.

Grandma and Grandpa were also known around the area for raising certified seed. If ever I complained about a tedious task like sweeping up feathers that would just reappear the next day, Mom took the opportunity to tell me how Grandma used to sit for hours combing through piles of seed and picking out undesirable kernels that would have degraded the quality of their product. Talk about tedious! Her tenacity and stubbornness seemed to come with a healthy dose of perfectionism. Luckily for us, eggs are larger than kernels of seed.

Grandma and Grandpa Otte also had a chicken house with hens laying more eggs than their family could eat. As she did with most everything in her life, Grandma tended her flock very carefully to promote maximum egg production for local sale. She and Grandpa Otte even kept the chicks in her basement to protect them from predators and the elements until they were strong enough to be turned out to the chicken house. My own mother learned a thing or two from Grandma about tending chickens. Little did she know that chickens would later become her whole life and that she would likewise teach her own children to tend chickens, albeit on a significantly larger scale.

Grandma's contributions to the farm were greater than just manual labor. Her keen eye for business, impeccable organizational skills, and careful study of various aspects of the agriculture industry gave them an advantage. All those records she so carefully kept came in handy as she compared her own notes with newspaper reports on things like pricing or seasonal supply-and-demand trends. According to the stories, Grandma's sharp mind and careful planning were somewhat of a secret weapon in sale barns, with her market savvy helping them decide which day was best to sell their hogs for the greatest profit.

The money she earned from selling her eggs was most often used for payments on a life insurance policy they had taken out on Grandpa Otte. Additionally, a small inheritance she received from her parents was put back into the farm. In 1951, Grandma used her $2,170 inheritance to buy an Oliver 66 Row-crop Tractor and install running water in the house.

If I thought it was tough sharing a single bathroom with my parents and siblings, I can't imagine how tough it would have been before they got indoor plumbing!

Before this tractor purchase, Grandma and Grandpa had exclusively farmed using mules, and they were one of the last in the area to switch to mechanized 'tractor' farming. Considering she was as stubborn as a mule, I'm not surprised she hung onto them so long. But this new tractor was instrumental in improving productivity and bringing the farm into a new and more competitive age of agricultural technology.

In 1967, just after I was born, Grandpa Otte died unexpectedly of a stroke. A seemingly very healthy and active man, everyone around was surprised when he passed so suddenly. Grandma had anticipated at least 20 more years of working side-by-side with him on the farm, as she had for more than three decades. He had only just signed up for a church bowling league with Zion Lutheran Church and had recently traveled to the Soviet Union for several weeks with some fellow farmers.

As devastating as his death was, Grandma at least felt secure in the fact that she had the farm and therefore a way to care for herself financially for her remaining years. She valued her independence and ability to dictate the terms of her life and potential success. No wonder this yearning for independence and dedication to personal success is so deeply ingrained in my being. It's been growing for generations!

That feeling of security and independence Grandma felt came to a screeching halt when the government contacted her. The IRS insisted that Grandma owed them money—a "widow tax"—saying that her inheritance from her parents was the only thing that had really belonged to her. After decades of pouring her blood, sweat, tears, money, and genius into the farm that she and her husband both worked, she was being told that none of it was of "money or money's worth," and that none of it was hers.

On top of this ownership issue, Grandpa had gifted her a couple hundred acres of farmland, transferring it to her name on advice from an attorney who was helping them with estate planning, a concept Grandpa had learned at a Farm Bureau meeting. Because the land gift had occurred just 15 months before his death, the IRS insisted that this land should be taxed with his estate because it constituted a gift given in contemplation of death and specifically to avoid impending estate taxes.

The whole situation had Grandma angrier than a wet hen. Obviously, Grandpa hadn't gifted that land to her in anticipation of dying unexpectedly of a stroke. Moreover, she rightly felt she was an equal partner in the farm in its entirety. She had contributed to every aspect of the farm every step of the way for the entirety of their marriage, and the taxes should reflect that.

The IRS insisted she owed $7,943.44, and Grandma could have put together the money and paid the tax, putting the whole thing to rest and moving on with what she had left. But even though that was a lot of money to come up with, that would have been taking the easy way out. As I can attest, that's just not in our genes. It was the principle of the matter, really. She knew this wasn't right and she wasn't about to be a chicken. She had faced the Great Depression and Mother Nature; she wouldn't cower before the IRS.

Grandma was whip smart, financially savvy, and very dialed into how things were in the community. She even had a subscription to The Wall Street Journal to keep herself informed, which was highly unusual for a woman in her position at the time, but she was always more than just a 'farm wife.' Grandma knew that farm wives were working the farms alongside their husbands, and she knew that when those husbands died, the wives were being taxed like she was. Because farming has limited liquidity, she knew widows were being forced to sell off some of their land to pay those taxes, reducing their property and limiting their independence. That didn't sit right with a tenacious woman so keen on creating her own success and protecting what she had spent her whole life working for.

She took up the fight not only for herself, but for hard-working farm widows around the country, past and future. She went to court to prove that she was an equal partner and contributor on the farm, both financially and through time, labor, and intellect. She presented her case regarding the gift of the land, as well as her equal partnership for tax purposes. Because she had been such a meticulous record keeper, she had all the receipts from her egg sales and her subsequent purchases for farm equipment, which she presented as evidence. I can just picture Grandma carrying shoeboxes full of receipts, smiling over loaded arms as she marched into the courthouse to win her case and make history.

Ultimately, in a landmark case, the United States Tax Court ruled in her favor. The judges agreed that Grandpa Otte was in "robust health" when he gifted the land to grandma, which meant it was not a gift made in anticipation of his death. Instead, they decided that the transfer was made "to avoid difficulties that may arise from property in joint names" and "was part of his estate plans but not merely to avoid death taxes."

The judges also commented on Grandma's partnership in the farm, saying, "Lura's efforts, industry and skill were not limited to those of an ordinary housewife. In our opinion such activity fairly justifies a division of property accumulated during her marriage for estate tax purposes."

Grandma was certainly no "ordinary housewife." Or perhaps, an "ordinary housewife" is a heck of a lot more impressive than this dismissive colloquialism would have you believe. She was a trailblazer with an incredible work ethic and unwavering commitment to her goals. She went to bat to fight an injustice that was affecting hardworking women around the country, and she reminded citizens that our government exists to serve us, not the other way around, something I think we all need to remember.

The ruling in her case set a national precedent regarding death taxes and the tradition of the IRS assuming that gifts are made in anticipation of death. She proved that a so-called "ordinary housewife" can be an equal partner, paving the way for wives and career women to be treated equally when they share responsibility, property, and wealth with husbands.

Who knows how many widows were able to keep their farms because Grandma was willing to fight for what she knew was right even though it would have been easier not to fight at all. She knew that what was happening was wrong and she knew she could bring about a change that would protect so many from a powerful governmental entity which often steamrolls the little guys.

This also set a family precedent I hold in high regard. She didn't just pass on a genetic propensity for tenacity, dedication, stubbornness, and an impressive work ethic. She lived them out, thereby teaching me what those character traits look like in real life. She showed me what it means to do the right thing even when it's hard. She proved to me the value of protecting those who might not be able to protect themselves. She taught me that while a responsible government is important to a civilized society, the American government is supposed to serve the people.

In my own life, I've faced obstacles and controversy that have tempted me to choose the easy way. Sometimes, doing what's right seems like harder work than farming in the 1930s, and hers are big shoes to fill. But I am committed to following in Grandma's footsteps and always doing what's right as I stand up for the little guy, both fellow farmers and hardworking citizens across the nation.

I've had to learn a lot of hard life lessons as I've tried to fill her shoes, but there's no better place to learn those lessons or build strong character than on a farm. So that's just what I did.

3

THE GREAT BLIZZARD

MOTHER NATURE HAS BEEN one of my greatest educators, and I haven't always enjoyed the lessons. The winter of '77-'78 was one of the coldest on record in Indiana and even the entire eastern half of the country, as arctic air masses relentlessly howled southeastward out of Canada. There were many winter storms during those months, but the Great Blizzard of January 26th, 1978, is permanently etched in my memory. It was different, and I am different because of it.

Looking back, I would consider my childhood rather idyllic, even with the amount of work I progressively received. Even at a young age, Dad would drop off my brother and me a mile from home so we could pick up litter as we walked back to the house after church. He always encouraged us to work hard not only for ourselves or even our farm, but also for others, including our community.

My responsibilities around the farm were ramping up and I was no longer just helping out. I certainly considered myself an essential contributor to the company and I had important duties in the large chicken houses at Jen Acres, and the smaller hand-gathered chicken houses at our P1 and P2 farms. While I spent endless hours sweeping aisles and collecting eggs, those weren't my only chores. In farming, we're all a team, and I was often expected to pitch in on unexpected tasks like using a four-foot-long brass grain probe to sample corn coming in from local farmers and used to feed our chickens, or holding air operated pneumatic levers at the feed mill to help weigh feed ingredients.

Whether it was picking up litter or working on the farm, there was always work to do, but all these tasks paled in comparison to this life-or-death blizzard that required all-hands-on-deck.

Temperatures began dropping ahead of the incoming blizzard. Every good Midwesterner knows to leave the water dripping when temperatures drop below zero so your pipes don't freeze, and the risk to our pipes was even greater as they were out in massive barns, not a cozy fire-warmed home. What's worse, it was getting dark. Hens don't drink much water at night, meaning the water was flowing like chilled molasses.

By nightfall, the temperature dipped well below zero. It was out of our control; the pipes began to freeze.

This not only risked expensive damage to the infrastructure of the hen houses if a pipe would burst, but it also risked the lives of our 10,000 hens who depended on us to keep them safe and healthy, and on whom we depended for financial stability. Those hens needed water, and we were the only way they were going to get it.

We bundled up and headed outside to begin what would become one of the longest nights of my life. I wasn't mentally prepared for the task that lay ahead, but sometimes the greatest lessons are learned when you're simply thrown in and forced to sink or swim. Luckily, I wasn't out there alone. I was part of a team working hard together to take care of those that depended on us.

We drove through the drifting and blowing snow to the hen houses at P1, getting out of the car with propane torches in freezing hand. I was nearly knocked on my 10-year-old rear from the whipping wind. I didn't think it could blow any harder than that, but as the night progressed, that's exactly what it did.

During the day, hen houses are considerably noisy, with chickens cackling and mechanical feeders clicking away, as the 600-foot flat chains that loop up and down the length of both sides of the hen houses carefully bring feed to the hens. At night, the hen houses are eerily quiet. The deadly silence of that evening was broken up by the howling winds outside. To this day, that sound rings loudly in my memory as Mother Nature was just outside roaring to be let in.

The metal roof creaked and groaned under the violent tear of wind. Around midnight, I looked up at the rafters, certain they would give way to the pressure at any moment and come flying off the top of the barn. There was very little conversation as the task before us required everyone's focus. Success was obligatory. If we didn't act quickly, the pipes would be lost, and thus the water supply.

I spent the whole night creeping along the 300-foot-long metal water line that was situated atop the 'roost' where hens would eat, sleep, and drink when not laying eggs. Crouched down with the propane torch, I heated the freezing metal water pipe from one end of the hen house to the other.

My legs and arms began to cramp from squatting so long, moving so slowly, and holding the torch. Caution was at the forefront of my mind as I heated the pipe, as I certainly didn't want to accidentally set fire to a sleeping hen. I stayed as quiet as possible so as not to wake them. Their laying schedule was paramount to our business' success; waking the hens could upset their body clock.

The hens would wake around five to lay. Having water flowing by that time was essential. As the pipes began to thaw, I desperately wanted a break, but Mother Nature showed no sign of stopping. So, neither did we.

My hands were numb. My legs were cramping. I had no choice but to keep pressing on. The only momentary relief I received was when changing propane canisters, but there was no time to delay. As soon as they were changed, it was back to work.

After an entire night working together in that frigid barn, the hens awoke. They started to drink, keeping water flowing in the pipes and preventing refreezing. As we stood to stretch our exhausted bodies, I had but a moment to appreciate the impact of all that work. The hens were healthy, the pipes were undamaged, and I had helped make that happen.

Even as I heaved a sigh of relief and satisfaction, there was more work to be done. The hens were awake now, which meant they were laying eggs. Many thousands of eggs. School was obviously out because of the blizzard, and farm hands who might have helped gather eggs were snowed in. I stood there staring down the 300 foot chicken nest boxes I had just squatted next to all night, thinking about how all those eggs would have to be gathered by someone. And then I realized— that someone was going to be me.

Gathering eggs from 10,000 chickens is a full-time job for one person. We had a cart that ran along a ceiling rail through the length of the hen house on both sides of the roost, which we would push along as we collected eggs from each nest. Typically, a hen in each nest would be sitting on her own egg, plus 2-4 more from other hens that had laid eggs in the nest earlier in the day. I would have to carefully reach my hand into the nest and slide it under the sitting hen to carefully gather the eggs from beneath her.

After enduring a frigid night that threatened the chickens, it was nice to feel the warmth of the freshly laid eggs in my bare hands. Many of the 'professional' and older egg gatherers typically wore gloves with the ends of the fingers cut off, which protected their hands from angry claws and beaks while allowing the eggs to be easily grasped by the bare fingers.

To my dismay, gloves were not a luxury we kids got to enjoy. I always tried to be careful not to scare or upset the sitting hen as I gathered the eggs under her because the last thing I wanted to deal with was a hen pecking my hands. To add insult to injury, the hens didn't seem to care that I had just worked the entire night to keep them alive.

Caring about their attitude wasn't an option. The hens and I were equally unimpressed with each other that day, but we depended on them just like they depended on us, so I had to buckle down and get to work. The eggs had to be gathered, and that was that. It was a huge and time-consuming job that I was responsible for, and I simply did not have time to worry about anything other than that. The protective and irritated hens would peck or even bite the back of my hand as I reached under them, but I was committed. So I gritted my teeth and reached in time and time again.

As I gathered the eggs, I placed them directly onto the paper flats of 30 eggs each that were on the rolling cart, even as I was already reaching for the next batch. There was no pausing for a break, and I was bone-tired when I reached the end of that long chicken house. But when I turned around and looked back at the seemingly endless row of now-eggless chicken nests, I was proud. Exhausted, but proud.

I had worked all night with everyone to keep those chickens safe and those pipes undamaged, then I had worked all day to gather the fruits of the hens' labor. I was literally pushing a cart full of eggs that were tangible evidence of my hard work, commitment, and ultimate success in the face of what seemed at the time to be insurmountable obstacles. The plate of eggs I scarfed down once I got back home never tasted so good.

As I look back on what seemed to be a particularly difficult day, I realize there were actually many others just as difficult. In fact, we repeated this whole pipe-thawing ordeal for several nights during that blizzard as temperatures remained low. We certainly weren't the only farmers dealing with the effects of such dangerously cold weather, and it certainly wasn't the last time I'd gather eggs from 10,000 hens in a day and come away with sore hands. When you're taking care of animals, you don't get the luxury of taking snow days off to sit back and relax.

I've since spent my life working as part of our company's team, responsible for many others. Whether it be animals, employees, or customers across the country, I've learned that when others are depending on me, I can and will show up, no matter how difficult it may be. Just as importantly, I've learned that hardworking teams of community-minded people are capable of overcoming the most gigantic obstacles.

The work I did during that blizzard was some of the hardest I remember from my childhood. Luckily, I didn't have to learn about hard work or teamwork from only difficult experiences. I also got to learn it from watching the overall management of the business.

One of the top requirements to build a successful business is hiring quality employees who consistently show up to do good work to advance business goals. Unfortunately, no one is as dedicated to your goals as you are, and that could mean trouble when building a company, especially one that requires difficult manual labor. But Dad was determined to encourage employees to work hard and foster a sense of commitment to the success of the company. He didn't want it to simply be a group of people who happened to work together. He wanted to build a community. So, back in the '60s, he devised a rather brilliant plan.

We called it the White Car Plan. Essentially, any employee who had attained seniority and didn't miss work for a certain amount of time got to collect a monthly bonus of $100 to use for monthly payments on a brand-new white automobile. This plan was not only a successful incentive for productivity, but everyone who saw these white cars driving around town knew the driver must be a quality employee at a company that valued them, which fostered pride and commitment to the community within the company.

To qualify for this bonus, an employee had to have perfect work attendance. To collect it, they had to attend one of our Saturday or Monday Night Meetings where they participated in discussions about management goals, farm performance, and various departments and tasks within the company.

While these discussions addressed arising issues, they were generally focused more on highlighting positive performance and accomplishments in the various departments. This encouraged improvement in the areas that were lacking. It was an important and earned responsibility, which both motivated employees and benefited the company. It meant that these committed company employees had a chance to contribute their unique insights and ideas to both the business and the team.

Dad saw almost everything as an opportunity to foster personal growth and improvement in himself, his children, and his employees. He was a big proponent of Dale Carnegie and the use of public speaking, so he expected every participant of these Saturday or Monday Night Meetings to write a letter to anyone and on any subject that mattered to them, which they would then read aloud to the whole group. Because attendance was how they got their bonus, and they had to write a letter if they were attending, there ended up being a flurry of letters written and read.

This was one of the most interesting and inspiring ideas Dad had for the business, and it wasn't even really about the business. It was about the people. Dad made sure I knew that people are what matter most. I spent my Saturday nights listening to letters written on every possible subject to every possible hypothetical recipient, be it relatives, friends, coworkers, community leaders, politicians, newspapers, or even sports teams. Whatever was on their mind or whatever they were most passionate about, this was their opportunity to publicly voice their opinion on the matter. Most often, the letters were team or community-minded in some regard, making these meetings akin to a college civics course.

While some of the letters were humorous or had unexpected subjects, all of them were interesting. It was inspiring to see these people stand with confidence and speak with power about things that were meaningful to them. I developed a deep appreciation not only for the privilege but also the practice of voicing personal opinions and insights, especially to contribute positively to the world we live in. To this day, I appreciate dialogue and conversation even with those who might hold views or opinions that do not match my own, a privilege we enjoy in this nation where our opinions and words are valued and protected.

Whether it be picking up litter on the side of the road, gathering eggs in a blizzard, or reading letters in a meeting, hard work and contribution from each individual helps achieve goals. Dad made this clear both at home and in the company, demonstrating what it meant to help make the world a better place for everyone.

While that starts with bettering ourselves, it doesn't end with us. To this day, two decades after my father died, I still run into people who remark on the impact Dad had on them or the impact they've since had on the world around them because of Dad's legacy.

Unfortunately, not everyone we meet has a positive impact on us, and not every group is community minded. Some even seek to do us harm. But those lessons are often incredibly valuable in their own right. And in coming years, I would learn some of those lessons, too.

4

THE SACRED DUTY OF CARE

GROWING UP ON A farm is often extremely hard and very dirty work. But as teens, we still had places to go and fun things to do. When I was 16 years old, my big brother got a brand spanking new 1983 Dodge Mirada. It was a beautiful white car with a red crushed velvet interior and an imitation convertible top.

For some reason that I'm sure he's forever regretted, my brother let me drive his new car to an after-church family lunch at The Pines, which has been the traditional spot for a Sunday smorgasbord for folks in Jackson County, Indiana for over 70 years. That day, I feasted on the usual buffet of fried chicken (this restaurant was one of the very first in the nation to be a licensee of Colonel Sanders' Kentucky Fried Chicken), along with fried fish, roast beef, ham, and more casseroles, salads, vegetables, breads, and desserts than I could possibly fit on a single plate.

After the usual amazing food and visiting with friends and neighbors at the restaurant, I got back in my brother's new Mirada and headed home. As I drove, I listened to songs on the radio. Whether it was a new Mellencamp song (John Mellencamp was from Seymour and his songs dominated the radio) or someone else, there was usually something good on.

Looking back and forth between the road and the radio, I began adjusting the controls on the new car. It only took a split second for my mistake to be punished; the next time I looked up at the road, I found myself staring directly at the brake lights of a car stopped on the road about 40 feet in front of me. I slammed on the breaks as fast as I could, but it was too late. I smashed directly into the other vehicle, totaling both cars.

Stumbling out of the vehicle, injured and bewildered, I was horrified to discover that the occupants of the car I hit were none other than a preacher and two older ladies. They promptly got out of the car and fell to their knees, offering up prayers for my comfort and well-being. While my injuries were ultimately minor—bruised ribs and one broken from the seatbelt that likely saved my life—prayer was the one thing they knew they could do to help a young man in pain.

The craziest part of all was that they didn't hold it against me. I was forgiven! Sure, I received a serious tongue lashing from Mom and Dad, and my big brother vowed I'd never touch anything he owned ever again, but both my family and that pastor were quick to show mercy. I was in the wrong, I made a terrible mistake, but I was forgiven.

They showed me the importance of compassion for others and taught me to see the good in those around me, even if they wronged me, which deeply influenced my personal life and extended throughout my career and in life. Seeing the good in the community has helped me build bridges where mistakes threaten to tear them down, make friends where differences might divide, and seek peace where anger risks conflict. Perhaps it was this very confidence in the good of society that caused me to be so profoundly affected by an animal rights activist terror attack on the family farm.

Up to that time, we in America would often hear of the tragedies of terroristic activity, but most never experienced it firsthand. It's difficult to appreciate the impact of a direct and targeted attack specifically intended to terrify and destroy until the target is you. That's exactly what the Animal Liberation Front (ALF) did to Rose Acre Farms, and I found myself deeply disturbed by the utter lack of goodness.

The ALF is an underground, decentralized, and leaderless animal rights activist movement that encourages direct action against those they deem guilty of engaging in any animal-related behaviors, businesses, or goals that the radical activists don't like. It's entirely subjective, allowing the activists to play judge, jury, and executioner. They carry out their illegal acts of property damage and sabotage in secrecy to avoid detection or identification.

On a dark and muggy July night, less than 1,000 feet from the home where I grew up, a large Rose Acres feed truck filled with food for tens of thousands of chickens in the adjacent hen houses was parked and waiting to be unloaded at the farm the next morning. Cloaked in darkness, radical activists from the ALF trespassed onto our land and spray painted a threatening message on the side of the feed mill: "POLLUTER, ANIMAL EXPLOITER, YOUR TURN TO PAY!." The truck used to transport all the feed to the nearby farm was set on fire, filling the night with the roar and orange glow of the inferno.

To make matters worse, they had also shot out a transformer carrying electricity to the farm, which immediately cut off the power to the fans used to ventilate the barns. Lack of air circulation could have led to the death of all our chickens in those barns, as the heat was stifling. Fortunately, the backup generators kicked in and no birds suffocated as a result of the attack.

While the saboteurs were too cowardly to operate in the light, the ALF radicals were proud of what they had done and publicly took credit for the blaze that destroyed the truck, ultimately totaling over $100,000 in damage. But it wasn't the burned truck that we cared about. It was the health and safety of our family, our employees, and of course, our chickens.

Everyone at Rose Acres was deeply affected by the aggressive attack so close to our home and our barns full of chickens. Employees and family members alike lived for quite some time in fear that the criminals would return, doing way more than just property damage. While working to care for our chickens and provide eggs to people across the nation, we all felt compelled to look over our shoulder, terrified of who might be lurking around the side of a barn, or hiding in the shadows of farm equipment. But if some of Mother Nature's harshest blizzards couldn't stop us from doing what needed to be done to care for our chickens, then neither could a rag-tag group of angry activists.

Frankly, Rose Acres had (and still has) a stellar reputation in the egg business. We've always been one of the very best, not only in terms of product quality but also in caring for our facilities, employees, and most particularly, our chickens. They are quite literally the lifeblood of the company. As stalwart guardians of the animals that depended on us for health and well-being, we took umbrage that these ideology-imposing criminals would burn a feed truck.

Did they not see the horrifying irony? Radical animal rights activists attempting to send a message about supposed animal cruelty by destroying this truck, thus causing significant harm and distress to thousands of the very animals they claimed to care about by leaving them hungry for hours until a new load of feed could be delivered from another county? Not to mention the fact that they all could have suffocated in the heat without ventilation, had we not had backup generators ready.

It was sheer evil to harm innocent and vulnerable chickens in the name of a social message. In fact, our mortification that they would harm our chickens in this way was almost as impactful as the fear their attack evoked.

After giving so much of ourselves for so many years to care for our chickens, we truly valued them. They were never just some meaningless thing that happened to be part of the business. They are the living, breathing cornerstone of the company that has been our life. We have never taken that lightly. Not even when the chickens belonged to someone else.

Back in the mid '90s, it was my usual job to go from farm to farm looking over facilities, but most importantly, talking to folks on the farms to be aware of how things were going, a job which I held until very recently. As an owner of the farm, I wasn't going there to order people around. I was really there to make sure everyone knew that we in the family cared deeply about them, their work, and their lives, as well as the lives of the chickens under our care.

Any business is only as good as its people. Because a flock of chickens can lay eggs 7 days a week, 365 days a year, we have no days off. Eggs that are laid must be collected, washed, inspected, and cartoned every single day. If a day were to be skipped, chaos would ensue in the barns. Eggs would pile up in a gigantic mess that you don't even want to imagine, much less have to clean up.

Because the folks at our company have to work holidays and weekends, I've always felt it was important to also be on the farms those days. For nearly 30 years, I have traveled to all our farms in 7 states every month. It was extremely important to me that I be on the farms at least a few Sundays and holidays a month, even in our most remote locations, to let the folks know that I care and appreciate that they are there.

I always knew that they were likely missing more than a few Sunday church services or after-church smorgasbords to care for our chickens, and therefore so did I. The important thing wasn't to try to catch someone doing something wrong, rather to catch someone doing something great. There is perhaps no greater satisfaction in life than to be 'caught' doing a phenomenal job at the work you love and to which you give your life. Most of the folks at our farms absolutely love what they do, and we love them for it, as they are essential to keeping the hens healthy.

We have many employees who have been with us for 10, 20, 30, 40, or even 50 years. It's because they know that in a family business, the family is working with them. We are a team. As I said before, the term 'employee' has simply never felt right. Early on, our Chief Operating Officer Tony Wesner instituted the term "team member" because on our farms, we are indeed all on the same team, caring for our flocks and striving to produce a food product that is essential for millions of people in America and around the world.

Driving home from one of my countless trips to Iowa, my brother called me up about a farm that we might be able to buy. As we were always expanding our operations, we were searching for either a location to build or an existing facility to purchase, which led us to discovering this chicken farm in Knob Noster, Johnson County, Missouri. I immediately changed course and drove directly to the farm to inspect it for potential purchase.

Initially, I was rather impressed with how clean the outside of the farm was, and how the hen houses appeared, especially considering farms are very dirty places if not run correctly. But as I stepped into the open doors of the barn, I was hit with a sickening smell that I knew was from animals who were not being cared for properly. Looks can be deceiving.

It wasn't the unpleasantness of the odor that disgusted me. It was knowing what was causing it. This was the smell of starvation.

I immediately knew I would find the feeders empty, which I did. I quickly ascertained that the owners of the farm were out of money. When they didn't have enough funds to buy grain to feed the chickens, they simply instituted a "skip-a-day" feeding plan, providing barely enough food to keep the hens alive. This lack of food was inducing a partial molt for the entire farm.

Molting is a healthy and natural thing and can be especially beneficial for older hens who need a "revitalization." As a hen gets older, the quality of her shells decreases, getting progressively thinner. The pause in laying during molting gives her body a break from the perpetual egg production that is natural for chickens. But these hens were molting as a result of their bodies prioritizing essential life-sustaining functions over egg production. Their little bodies were literally shutting down.

There is a distinctive odor associated with molting, which I know from the many natural and healthy molts I've witnessed by our own chickens. But stress-molting is different, and the smell of stress-molting permeated each of the 12 chicken houses I inspected on this farm. To my dismay, I saw that almost all the chickens on the entire farm had no food.

Very quickly, we had closed a deal to buy the farm at a bankruptcy sale and had already coordinated to have feed delivered to the starving chickens at the soonest possible opportunity. As farmers and caregivers for millions of hens, there was never a single second of thought about getting those chickens fed. It was a given from the moment I entered those barns.

It's rather insulting that radical activists like the Animal Liberation Front would think we're not doing everything in our power to care for the animals who depend on us, and on whom we depend. No matter the difficulty we faced, or whether people treated us poorly, we would never stop doing our best to treat others and our chickens with the respect and care they deserve. This sacred duty of care was ingrained in me as a young boy and continues to influence my decisions today, both when dealing with chickens and my fellow man. I want my legacy to be one of a man on whom others could always depend.

As our chickens, employees, and customers across the nation depend on us, Rose Acres had to find a way to continue operating the farms in the face of significant obstacles, including increasing regulations and hostility, even if it made things more difficult for us. And things would definitely become more difficult.

5

CONTAGION

I'M NOT AFRAID OF much, including facing difficult challenges. Mom and Dad preferred what might now be called "free-range parenting," allowing me to learn by suffering the natural consequences of my own decisions. It made me resilient and rather fearless in the face of obstacles or opponents.

But there is one thing that strikes fear into every egg farmer on the planet—Bird Flu.

Avian Influenza, or Bird Flu, is a viral infection that primarily affects birds. It is transmitted through direct contact with infected birds or their droppings, or even people who carry it from infected birds to other healthy birds. In America, it is most often contracted from goose excrement. When flying south for the winter, they can drop infected feces on top of chicken houses, which can then be sucked into the ventilation system so that the hens breathe in the virus, even if it was just a fleck of infected feces.

If even a single bird in a barn contracts the virus, it spreads like wildfire through an entire chicken house, killing thousands or even potentially millions of birds within days and causing production to plummet, which means that strict bio-security measures must be rigorously followed. Some may find them extreme, but it is an inconvenient truth that if the egg industry is to survive a bout of Bird Flu, certain measures must be taken.

We do not allow anyone that works on our farms or that visits our farms to have pet birds, chickens, or fowl of any kind. Bird Flu can be easily spread by humans from backyard flocks to large commercial operations simply by bringing in some bird droppings stuck to a shoe. In fact, we even have to disinfect the tires of every vehicle entering our farms, lest they inadvertently bring infected feces onto the property, which can then be stepped in and tracked into the hen houses. Additionally, all employees and visitors must wear protective clothing even after disinfecting their shoes.

Employees who work directly with the hens must "shower in" and "shower out" to sanitize every person and piece of clothing that crosses the threshold of the hen houses. These rules are followed extremely rigorously, and the violation of these rules results in dismissal, as it can have devastating effects.

As Chairman of the Board for the company, I would dread every phone call from our farms during the times that the Avian Influenza was striking across the United States. My worst fear in those days was that I'd answer and hear the words, "We have a confirmed case of Bird Flu." That statement alone would predict the potential death of millions of laying hens. It would increase the burden on employees and threaten their job security, as many other farms may lay off employees during a Bird Flu outbreak, although we never do. It would also mean suffering for consumers, who would have fewer eggs to be able to buy. Other than praying, there would be very little I could do to help, no matter how much I wanted to. And I always wanted to.

While we care deeply for the hens that are the lifeblood of our business, unfortunately, Avian Influenza requires that the entire farm's flocks be humanely euthanized to prevent the total devastation of the egg industry.

We have endured many years of this horrific illness, and I've received the dreaded phone call several times. But during the horrific 2022 Bird Flu season, the call I got was truly gut-wrenching—we had a confirmed case in a chicken house at our farm in Guthrie Center, Iowa. In the blink of an eye, one case turned into hundreds of thousands.

My heart sank as I knew that we would have to remove every chicken on the farm to try to stop the spread. On top of that, I knew the burden this would place on the employees and the nation's egg supply.

Over 1.5 million chickens were carefully taken from their cages and immediately euthanized with CO_2, then disposed of under strict regulations, to protect other birds from being infected. In years prior, our farms at Winterset and Stuart, Iowa had also been wiped out. We went to great lengths to once again disinfect an entire farm so that a new flock could be brought in. I was devastated that we were going through this again.

When an entire flock is wiped out, the long-term plan for the entire farm is thrown into a frenzy. We can't just order one or two million new laying hens overnight from our local farm supply store. It takes about 17 weeks from hatching for a hen to be able to lay eggs, and each chicken only lays one egg at a time, usually just 5 eggs per week, per hen. We'd need 1.6 million! When Avian Influenza hits, the number of birds being lost to the virus vastly outpaces the number of eggs being laid to hatch new laying hens, leading to a lag in available supply to replace lost flocks and prolonging the crisis for farmers and consumers.

Have you ever noticed a sudden spike in egg prices or poultry? This is often related to a Bird Flu breakout. With increased costs for the farms, combined with reduced sellable eggs, consumers end up with a higher price tag. This spells disaster for farms like Rose Acres who prioritize affordable food for American consumers.

Worse than the cost of replacing entire flocks or the added expenses to implement the rigorous bio-safety protocols, many people depend on our farm for a job. On top of that, we can't afford to lose good team members with valuable experience and industry knowledge. We need them immediately ready when new hens arrive, so we pay them to clean all the facilities even when there are no hens on the farm in an effort to keep them as team members who are ready to work. They are family to us and mean even more to us than our hens.

I have faced the rage of Mother Nature before, but there really is nothing to be done in the face of such a highly contagious virus. At least, not that we are allowed to do. Hack politicians are quick to pounce and blame price hikes on farmers. But it's the United States government and the bought-and-paid-for career politicians that are the culprit behind the high price of eggs during Avian Influenza. As Ronald Reagan said, "the nine most terrifying words in the English language are: I'm from the Government, and I'm here to help."

Bird Flu is preventable. There is a vaccine that is available in much of the world. But it is not in the United States. Our government bans the use of this vaccine here in America. Other developed countries inoculate their flocks against Avian Influenza and keep their hens healthy, preventing infection and subsequent drops in production or spikes in price. But the U.S. government is under pressure from China to not allow United States egg farmers to vaccinate their hens. It's all about establishment control, not preventing catastrophe. And who funds the establishment?

If we were permitted to utilize this vaccine, untold millions of hens over the years wouldn't have needlessly died, including 50 million hens in 2022 alone, when Bird Flu hit hard. The strain was so bad that even as chickens were swiftly dying of infection, millions of healthy birds had to be quickly killed in a desperate attempt to prevent spread.

Prices for a dozen eggs inevitably spiked to levels that almost reached the price of a large, fancy coffee at Starbucks! It was such big news that there were even memes about "expensive eggs!" People were outraged and farmers were automatically accused of price gouging. Interestingly, even at five bucks a dozen, when you adjust for inflation, eggs were still cheaper than they were back in the 1950s. Unfortunately, in this matter, we simply don't have any control. We're up against both Mother Nature and government regulations.

Free market capitalism has kept egg prices so low that people take it for granted, assuming they will always be an inexpensive staple on their grocery list. But were it not for the 70 years of effort by Rose Acres to mitigate price increases by building new and ever larger egg farms to keep eggs affordable, this would not be the case.

After the catastrophic Bird Flu outbreak of 2022, egg prices initially skyrocketed due to the widespread shortage. Despite having fewer chickens producing eggs, we were able to make enough money to get by. That money went directly into the pockets of our employees, who we always make sure are paid. It also went back into the business as we quickly invested in new hen houses and even an entire new farm to increase our egg production. From those first two 500-hen coops on the old Rust farm up to today, when we have over 21 million chickens, we've always put profits back into the business to improve efficiency, increase production, keep consumer costs low, and invest in the future.

During that 2022 epidemic, we did our part. The government perpetually refuses to do theirs. They continue to prohibit a precautionary measure that could have prevented the entire 50 million-hen catastrophe and the subsequent egg price spike. Vaccinating the birds would have kept the egg supply constant in 2022.

Frustratingly, it's the farmers who take the brunt of the public outrage and accusations of harming consumers. Only a year later in 2023, we faced another bout of Bird Flu, and yet again, farmers were being blamed. Despite doing everything possible in the face of Mother Nature's viral rage while being handcuffed by a controlling government, somehow, farmers are made out to be the bad guys who are driving up egg prices.

Why don't the Washington elites want the flocks vaccinated, even though they know it would avoid a crisis that negatively impacts the American people? One reason is that selling to China is more important to them than protecting the egg market in America. Despite vaccinating their own flocks, China refuses to buy poultry from countries that vaccinate against Avian Influenza, even as they vaccinate against it themselves. They are counting on America risking the decimation of our flocks and the spiking of our egg market to comply with China's hypocritical demands that unnecessarily raise food prices for the American consumer. And that's exactly what our government makes the egg market do.

This is a rather obvious ploy by an enemy nation to force avoidable economic turmoil upon America, and our government has played right into their hands. The Chinese government clearly doesn't actually care about consuming vaccinated poultry, as they vaccinate their own chickens to prevent the very decimation of their own flocks and the price hikes of their own egg market that they force on us. Their goal is an angle of control over America. How terrifying that our own government would rather capitulate to the demands of China than protect our own national interest of having a healthy and economical food that we all love!

I suspect another reason they don't allow farmers to vaccinate flocks is the same reason they don't really want a security wall built at our southern border to address that similarly preventable crisis—if it gets done, they can't campaign on fixing the issue or go after the people they pretend to blame. I'm always shocked when Republicans have the ability to accomplish great things for this country, like in 2017-18 when we had control of the House, Senate, and White House, but then squander that opportunity.

If they build a complete border wall from the Pacific Ocean to the Gulf of Mexico, they can't vilify the Democrats for inviting and allowing the crisis, or promise their voters that they'll deal with the crisis. And if they allow farmers to vaccinate their hens, then they can't blame those farmers for the economic hardship the American people face today as a direct result of irresponsible and activist government spending.

That's the idiocy of career politicians in Washington on full display, and it's one of the many obstacles that American farmers unnecessarily face. Politicians refuse to do the things we all know could help, instead doing things that will harm, and then blaming everyone else for the consequences of their actions.

For example, during COVID, they shut down businesses, destroyed the economy, and devalued the dollar. They then blamed farmers when eggs inevitably became more expensive based on inflation and the devaluation of the dollar, which had nothing at all to do with the egg supply. It's the same with Bird Flu. They prohibit farmers from preventing a devastating disease that wipes out our flocks, then blame us when the price of eggs inevitably goes up.

Yet how many of the people who either allowed or actively exacerbated these issues are now campaigning on a platform of addressing those issues?

Career politicians and their corporate cronies are always looking for a scapegoat, and farmers often seem to have the displeasure of being chosen. Another prime example involves another pathogen.

Salmonella is a human and animal bacteria that can cause very severe illness, with human infection occurring most frequently through water or food that has been contaminated by infected human or animal feces. Some people with salmonella infection have no symptoms, while others can develop diarrhea, fever, and abdominal cramps within hours after exposure. However, most healthy people recover within several days without specific medical treatment.

Salmonella bacteria are ubiquitous to the human and animal environment, which means they are naturally found all around us—anywhere there is life and therefore fecal matter. Unless we happen to be in a sterile surgical environment, chances are that we'll find it if we swab the surfaces in our home, work, or community.

In the normal scope of life here in America, it isn't a huge concern, and it is easily avoided by sticking to rather basic food handling and preparation guidelines. Consuming raw or undercooked animal products increases the risk of getting sick, while proper washing, cooking, and refrigerating can kill or prevent the bacteria from multiplying. This is why food establishments are required to follow strict rules for hygiene, cooking, and food storage.

Back in the '90s, testing was developed for salmonella, which made the blame game that much easier. Even though salmonella bacteria can be anywhere around us (likely through the ages of history) and can be picked up and multiplied at every step in food preparation, it's rather easy to blame the farmers who are the ultimate source of food. That's exactly what happened to Rose Acres.

Before the turn of the century, a convention in a major Chicago hotel served a bread pudding from which 379 people became severely ill due to salmonella food poisoning. In looking for someone to blame, Rose Acres was targeted as the "source" of the outbreak, with claims that our farm had supplied the eggs that were used in the improperly prepared and stored bread pudding.

In the course of discovery over this incident, the use of our farm's shell eggs in the bread pudding was called into question altogether, as such a recipe was more likely to use a frozen (and then thawed) pasteurized egg product which was not made by our farm. It was speculated that the dish was allowed to 'set' overnight in an unrefrigerated and unheated environment, which would explain the sheer volume of bacteria present to make so many people so sick.

When these details were revealed, I wasn't the only one shocked. Even the thought made my stomach turn. Anyone with even minimal experience in a kitchen would be horrified to hear of so-called food professionals leaving raw or under-cooked food in a room temperature environment for hours, surely growing bacteria of all kinds, and then serving that veritable petri dish to unsuspecting crowds. It was a recipe for disaster, and we were the chosen scapegoat even though we didn't believe our eggs were used in the actual recipe at all.

Our White County Egg Farm chicken houses were tested for salmonella in an attempt to prove that we were to blame for the severe illness of hundreds of convention patrons. I wasn't the least bit surprised when the inspectors determined that salmonella bacteria were present in our chicken houses. As I said before, salmonella bacteria can be present almost anywhere—door handles, home and restaurant table-tops, menus, cellphones, shopping carts, and school desks. Anything a human or animal can touch. It wasn't surprising, nor was it proof. The salmonella in that bread pudding could have come from almost anything, and it could have easily been prevented through proper food handling, preparation, and storage.

Ridiculously, the inspectors only tested the hen houses for salmonella, never any of our eggs. Not a single one.

Over the years, we have been similarly blamed when incorrect food handling has caused illness, but we are dedicated to producing a quality and healthy product. Our farms have produced over 180 billion eggs for consumption—8 billion eggs per year—and not a single egg has ever tested positive for salmonella. While we're proud of this fact, that certainly doesn't mean you should ever consume foods with raw eggs, especially when that food has been grossly mishandled by humans that do human things, like use the bathroom. Cross contamination of bacteria and subsequent illness from human feces carried by improperly washed hands that are preparing food is unfortunately something that happens in an imperfect world.

Even if the egg is perfect.

Despite no testing of our eggs or proof that we were even the supplier for the product in question, we were blamed for the food poisoning and the government stepped in, forcing us to stop selling eggs from that farm on the retail shell egg market. We subsequently lost millions of dollars from this arbitrary and capricious implementation of food safety laws.

We knew we had done nothing wrong and that we weren't to blame, as we proudly maintain the highest standards for our farms and our eggs. It wasn't right to be punished just so someone could be blamed. I couldn't help but wonder how many other small businesses were similarly being crushed as scapegoats.

But if Grandma Otte taught us anything, it was that we never back down from a fight. We decided to defended ourselves and fought for what was right by suing the government in a U.S. Court of Federal Claims for unjustly blocking us from selling our eggs despite never having a single egg test positive for salmonella.

A judge ruled in our favor and ordered the government to pay us $6.1 million in damages, but the ruling was overturned on appeal and ultimately thrown out. The government doesn't like admitting when they are wrong, especially when it is hardworking people suffering because of it, whether through unnecessarily high consumer prices or small businesses being crushed.

These career politicians are so far removed from reality and from the hardworking people who are the backbone of this nation, they don't even realize how ridiculous their behavior must appear to the people who work for a living. Perhaps this is because they've lived soft and protected lives, rarely facing accountability or hardship, like having an entire farm decimated by a virus or your reputation threatened by bacteria. The moment anything gets uncomfortable for them, they virtue signal with meaningless votes that have no chance of ever passing while they point the finger to vilify someone else—anyone else—for whatever is angering people, whether it be high prices, illness, or lack of a border wall.

Farmers don't have that luxury. When things get hard, we have to deal with it head on, whether it's Mother Nature, radical activists, or our own government. Although it sure would be nice if our people in Washington understood anything about agribusiness or even hard work, as the American consumers wouldn't pay such a hefty price for the ignorance, or worse yet, the willful deception by the government.

While the cost of eggs was high in 2022 from Bird Flu, prices crashed in 2023 due to a massive egg surplus, with farmers losing money most of the year. But there was no cry for government handouts or massive messaging campaigns to deflect blame. We know that the free market will sort things out and we are strong enough to power through it. In fact, as Bird Flu hit in the fall of 2023 and early 2024, thirteen million hens have already had to be killed, once again driving egg prices up and spurring accusations of 'price gouging.' But hardworking and dedicated farmers know this is simply how the market works, and we don't do it for power, gain, or social acclaim.

We've been dedicated to our mission for more than 70 years and will continue to do so for at least another 70! Farmers will always farm, and it's our love of feeding America that helps us survive.

It's an incredible honor to be able to feed millions of people every day despite the many obstacles we face in doing so. Farmers expect to battle Mother Nature, and even radical activists and incompetent or leveraged politicians are no longer a surprise. But sometimes, our adversaries are a little more conniving in how they seek to control us, and we have had to adapt to those obstacles as well.

6

A LESSON IN FREEDOM

WHILE FARMERS ALWAYS FACE natural enemies like blizzards and viruses, our opponents were increasingly becoming entities beyond our incompetent government, who sought to undermine and restrict the success of agribusinesses like egg farms. The attack on our farm by the Animal Liberation Front in 2000 marked a new and difficult era for the company in which we would be forced to adapt to the growing industry regulations, outrage, and even violence levied against our company in a way that conflicted with our moral and ideological values. But lessons of survival can quite literally change lives—they certainly did mine.

My dad, David Rust, was a staunch believer in American free market capitalism. As a patriot and visionary, he considered this an essential part of the American Dream. The memories of my childhood are painted in shades of red, white, and blue, and I always knew that he valued freedom and opportunity more than almost anything else. That's why Dad was so opposed to joining egg industry associations back in the '70s and '80s. He was particularly worried that they would be used to inhibit free market capitalism within the farming and egg industry, and he was determined to protect our business, our family, and our customers.

In 1972, farmers in Canada had flocked together to form a marketing order for chicken farms and egg production. This was a legal agreement to control national flock size and therefore control the price of eggs to ensure that less committed and minimally successful farmers still made a profit. It's a governmental regulatory mechanism implemented by agricultural authorities to manipulate various aspects of a market to control the price of a product by also controlling the availability of that product. And Dad made sure I knew exactly how damaging this could be.

He took every opportunity to educate, and family meals were no exception. I remember many conversations around the dinner table about marketing orders, regulations, and government control. As a child, I understood these economic principles as well as I understood the fundamentals of taking care of chickens—feed, water, and air.

Dad explained that if regulators wanted to keep the price of eggs artificially high to generate the greatest profit for farmers, they would have to restrict production. This would stop new, larger, and more cost-efficient farms from being built, artificially keeping prices high for Canadians.

Since chickens produce eggs, and more chickens produce more eggs, forcing farmers to cap the number of chickens they could own would essentially constrain farmers to produce fewer eggs than a growing population needs. This restricts their availability on the market, thereby raising the monetary value, translating to a price increase for consumers.

This regulatory scheme is government sanctioned and perfectly legal (and even mandated) in Canada. It's also perfectly legal right here in the United States, so long as all the farmers involved are in a specific co-op created to strictly control the size of production with a similar aim as in Canada.

This didn't sit right with Dad. Dinnertime lessons weren't just about the dangers of marketing orders. He also impressed upon me how important free market capitalism is to success and opportunity. After all, it was why we had a family business in the first place. While it may sometimes hurt to let the market decide prices instead of allowing restrictive regulatory organizations to control them, it ultimately ensures the lowest price of eggs for the consumer.

Another major consideration of market orders is international sales, as a marketing order can prohibit free trade with other countries. Otherwise, those countries would come in and sell all their products, thus flooding the market and lowering the price. Because Canada has a strict marketing order, eggs from the United States cannot be legally sold in Canada.

This always seemed so bizarre to me. Politicians talk a big game about "free trade," but it's often a one-way street, especially with Canada. We allow Canadian automobiles to be sold in the United States, so why can't we sell our eggs in Canada? We would love to, for our own benefit and that of Canadian consumers, but we cannot. Ross Perot was completely correct when he warned of the "giant sucking sound" the North Atlantic Free Trade Agreement (NAFTA) would create—jobs being exported under the guise of "free trade" while hardworking Americans pay the price for that in terms of lower wages.

Many American egg farmers saw what the Canadian egg farmers were doing and wanted to go with production quotas here as well. That way they could work a little less hard but still be guaranteed a certain level of profit, even if consumers suffered. But Dad wasn't about to take the easy way out or unnecessarily burden his fellow Americans. He believed marketing orders and various other industry organizations were essentially a government-created and government-regulated price gouging conspiracy, and he didn't want that here in America.

It wouldn't be easy, but Dad knew he needed allies who understood the dangers these associations posed to free market capitalism. He was so determined that he even paid to fly other egg farmers to Indianapolis to meet with him in person to discuss the issue. He was sure that if he could talk to them and explain, they would stand with him against joining these marketing orders or other associations.

As a freshly licensed 16-year-old, my newest responsibility was to drive up to the Indianapolis airport to meet visiting egg farmers and bring them back to Seymour to meet with Dad. On one particular visit from a kind old farmer, I spent the whole drive chatting about our family history, our business, and why we were so dead set against these regulatory mechanisms. Dad had taught me well, and I voiced my strong opinion on the matter. I've always wondered what he thought of a teen boy discussing such a weighty subject. I'd like to think I sort of warmed him up for the conversation with Dad that was to come.

Ultimately, Dad was able to convince others to be wary of the temptation to create marketing orders, and people still remember the tenacity and stubbornness with which he fought this fight for what he knew was right. He stood up to pressure within the industry and told everyone who would listen exactly what he thought of marketing orders. He was extremely unpopular for a while, but I'm proud to have witnessed him almost single-handedly save the agricultural free market for both the egg farmer and consumer during that time.

Through the '80s and '90s, as I became more involved with the company, we managed to continue operating independently of other egg farms, just as dad had taught us. We rarely participated in industry organization events other than trade shows, specifically so we could avoid the taint of being associated with such anti-free market thinking. But the ALF attack changed things. It marked a significant increase in radical and even dangerous animal rights activism, fueling social outrage and bringing down incredible pressure on our retail customers.

We could no longer stand alone. We had to join an industry organization called the United Egg Producers (UEP). It was a matter of survival, not choice.

This was a difficult decision for the family. To my very core, I was opposed to the idea, especially in light of the many conversations I had on the subject, whether around the dinner table, working side-by-side with the family on the farms, or even driving in the car with visiting farmers. It made me uneasy knowing we were forced to do what Dad always taught us to defend against.

We had a figurative gun to our heads from massive corporate customers who were threatening to ice us out of the market entirely unless we joined and submitted to uniform and industry-dictated production standards. The principal issue was that the industry's biggest retail grocery store customers were refusing to buy eggs from any farmer that didn't fully comply with the new cage space regulations that were being imposed, in large part due to the increased activism and subsequent public outrage. Unfortunately, most consumers who thought this would be a universally good thing didn't realize the unintended consequences this could have on the industry and themselves.

Ultimately, it was mega-corporations that forced our hand by requiring us to join and comply with UEP regulations, specifically the cage space requirement, if we wanted to keep their business. Ironically, some of these same mega-corporations would later sue us for the natural market consequences of our company doing exactly what they demanded us to do.

From the start of the conversation about joining the UEP, I fought hard at the board level against it. I argued that we would face significant issues in the future from this decision, which we did. Joining such an organization could and would be painted as "bad" for one reason or another, even though we were being forced into it for our survival.

Our motives wouldn't matter. Changing industry and social whims would mean adversaries could use this against us if we relinquished some of our freedoms for this sense of security.

This move was especially upsetting to me personally as I didn't like 'giving in' to the animal rights terrorists who were pushing an agenda to eliminate egg production entirely, or to the mega-corporations who were pushing an agenda for their own profits. But as a farm, we had to survive to pay our employees. In the end, I reluctantly agreed.

The fact is that the university experts who helped the UEP set their science-backed guidelines for Animal Care Certification showed that increasing the cage space per chicken was the right thing to do for bird health. That was a huge consideration for me as I have always poured my heart and soul into caring for our chickens.

There were some other farmers that didn't join, perhaps for the same reasons we held out as long as we did. But they didn't last long outside the UEP. They came under so much pressure from their customer base that their decision was also one of business survival. There was no alternative. You can't survive in any business without customers.

My brother Marcus was very clear that adopting this particular regulation was the right thing to do for our survival, but we had to be very careful about how we adopted it so we didn't destroy our business or destroy the egg market for our customers. This was another major family decision.

We would join the United Egg Producers, but we would never go along with joining for the purposes of lowering the nation's egg supply to raise prices. To avoid the possibility of being accused of that, Marcus was adamant that we would immediately begin building new egg production infrastructure to increase our bird numbers and thus the national egg supply.

I was still very reluctant to join, but it had to be done. As I walked through hen houses with others from the company and family, we discussed what we would have to do. We had to consider all the costs, not just to our business but to employees and customers as well.

An obvious solution to someone who doesn't have experience with chicken farming would be to retrofit every single cage or pen to be bigger, making the chicken-to-cage space ratio compliant with regulations. However, with millions of cages, that's not remotely practical.

The only practical option would be to simply house fewer chickens in each cage until each chicken had the required space set forth by the university experts. But this meant many fewer chickens per chicken house, and that meant many fewer eggs being produced.

Despite this being the only practical option, we had two major concerns with this plan. First, fewer birds would mean fewer eggs, thus requiring fewer employees for both taking care of the hens and for processing and packaging the eggs. This could lead to layoffs. Second, it would mean that the price of eggs could go up as the availability of eggs would go down, unless new production was quickly added.

None of this felt right to us. My brother Marcus pushed hard for what would have to be done to allow us to be regulation compliant while keeping all our chickens and employees happy and busy, and help us mitigate a potential price spike for customers.

As we had so many times before, we decided to expand.

We were going to grab the challenge of complying with this regulation by the horns and make it work out for the consumer.

We embarked on what would end up being a decades-long project to enlarge our facilities and increase our flocks in almost every state where we operated. We built a new farm in North Carolina, adding over 3 million chickens with that one facility alone. We also added two new chicken houses with hundreds of thousands of chickens each to numerous facilities in Indiana, Iowa, Missouri, Illinois, and Georgia. While we were making existing houses regulation compliant for space, we were not only maintaining the size of the existing flocks, but actually adding more chickens than we had before.

This added nearly 6,500,000 more chickens overall to the nation's egg-laying flock, just from our own family's farms!

In the end, our plan helped grow our hen numbers to increase the supply of eggs for all Americans. And we got to keep all our team members on the payroll. Our choices, especially the difficult ones, were made with the best interest of hardworking Americans in mind. It was our neighbors and friends that we thought about every step of the way.

These days, you can drive by many of our farms and see the newer and larger houses built onto the ends of the previously existing farm facilities. They are massive and they are a reason eggs continue to be such an economical food for the American consumer. These new barns are a tangible reminder that we are willing to do what we know is right even when it requires extra work or creativity. But in business, as in life, no good deed goes unpunished.

7

NO GOOD DEED GOES UNPUNISHED

OUR WORLD IS FULL of inconvenient truths, like that we get wiser as we get older, and we sure could have used that wisdom when we were young and just starting out. I've had to learn about many of these truths while being on the more troublesome side of things. But I've never been one to shy away from truth just because it's inconvenient. Nor am I one to shy away from a fight with those who don't appreciate them. For me, it's always been, "speak the truth and shame the devil."

One such truth is that if people want to buy eggs easily and affordably from a store, those eggs have to be produced somewhere on a large scale. Some don't like that farms like ours exist, but if they didn't, where would people get their eggs?

Another is that making money is a necessary part of business, including egg farming. Otherwise, the business would cease to exist. This truth is particularly unpleasant to people who don't appreciate that our profits might take away from theirs, mainly greedy mega-corporations.

After surviving the potentially catastrophic anger of Mother Nature and attacks by radical activists who think our farms shouldn't exist at all, we continued to engage in many legal battles with corporations that seek maximum profit at any cost, no matter if the cost involved gets paid by the consumer. Perhaps the most terrifying aspect of the many legal battles we've fought over the years is the tactics used to undercut small businesses and hardworking Americans, ultimately threatening the essence of American free market capitalism and the American farmer.

The America my dad taught me to love and appreciate is slipping away. Once a land dedicated to freedom, opportunity, and equality, America has descended into a two-tier system that elevates select classes above the masses. There's a sinister symbiotic relationship between mega-corporations, politicians, and the lawyer class, with the success of each depending on mutual back-scratching.

The losers in the equation are the American people and small businesses, who are routinely crushed out of existence. As these elite classes control the system that perpetuates and reinforces their power, it's become a machine almost too big for the hardworking American to defeat. Almost. But it's still possible, and I was raised to face challenges head on and fight for what's right, even if that fight seems almost too big to win.

One way this powerful machine has seen such crushing success is by manipulating antitrust laws to ruin the very businesses these laws were intended to protect. Antitrust laws were instituted to ensure fair competition, prevent monopolies, and safeguard consumers from the concentration of economic power, allowing consumers to benefit from a variety of choices, competitive prices, and innovation.

In the hands of greedy corporations, sleazy lawyers, and their political cronies—literal monopolies—these laws have become a weapon against the very essence of the American dream—entrepreneurship and free enterprise.

A prime example of this reality is a lawsuit brought against Rose Acre Farms in 1988 by a group of egg farms desperate to sue a main competitor out of business. They alleged that our company was selling eggs too cheaply, causing their businesses to lose customers to ours. They used antitrust laws as their basis for trying to destroy us.

I was working my way through college when the lawsuit went to trial, and despite my course load and work schedule, I made sure I was at every single day of that trial. We all did. My mother, brothers, sisters, and I walked into that big classical Federal Courthouse building in downtown Indianapolis and watched every minute of their attempt to destroy us for producing our product at a cheaper price to benefit the consumer.

We spent hours in those courtroom chairs, watching one of the sleaziest lawyers I've ever met put on an impressive performance to bamboozle a jury who was all too eager to swallow his tale hook, line, and sinker. Rather short and dressed to the nines, their lawyer was a hot shot from Chicago. Through the whole trial, he and his team had the table loaded with stacks and boxes of paperwork. I remember very well how he constantly joked within earshot of the jurors (but not the judge) about how their table was going to collapse under the weight of all the evidence they had against Rose Acres. That "evidence" was really just the history of an American success story.

I was proud that we didn't need an unethical lawyer with theatrics and a carefully spun narrative. We didn't do anything wrong; we only did what any business would do. The business was growing quickly, and we needed to expand our customer base. We had to have the best price to entice new customers, so we pitched a lower price than some other farms did. Of course, the corporate customers appreciated the savings, and so did the consumers. But our competitors didn't like that their customers were buying from us for a better price.

Rather than improving their own companies to compete with Rose Acre Farms, these companies preferred to crush us out of existence with a courtroom battle and legal fees, forcing their corporate customers to buy from them for a higher price and making eggs less affordable for hardworking American consumers. They were using laws intended to protect consumers to instead harm them. They wanted these antitrust laws to protect them from competitors by claiming unfair competition.

As the trial came to a close, I was dismayed to see the jury completely hoodwinked by the lawyer's deceptive rhetoric. In an impressively anti-free market decision, the jury found us guilty. I feared for the future of American agriculture, economy, and opportunity. Was I watching the death of everything Dad taught me to appreciate?

Luckily for every hardworking and entrepreneurial American in the nation at that time and for generations to come, the judge saw through the lawyer's tactics and recognized the dangers of such a precedent. He threw out the jury's guilty verdict and wrote his own scathing verdict that rather comically used puns to address the fundamental lack of merit in the lawsuit, like saying that the evidence against us was "poultry," instead of using the word paltry.

As a family and a business, we were incredibly relieved to have won this legal battle for our right to engage in reasonable business practices that benefit both our company and our consumers, even if some of our competitors didn't appreciate our success. This trial had a profound impact on me, teaching me valuable lessons about the tendency to seek control at the expense of others and the need to fight for what is right instead of bowing to power.

Years later, when the courthouse underwent a refurbishment, I discovered that the old chairs from the courtrooms were up for sale. I purchased a dozen of the very chairs I had spent so many hours in, waiting on the edge of my seat to see if free market capitalism would be dealt a blow by colluding corporations and the lawyer class, or if American principles would win out in the end. These chairs, which I see every day in my office, continue to be a poignant reminder of the freedom and opportunity I will always fight to preserve.

But this antitrust lawsuit would be only one of many legal battles faced in the years to come. We realized fairly quickly that some people would rather pay to destroy their competition than work to elevate their own business. Free markets reward hard work, but not everybody is willing to work hard.

After many decades working to make Rose Acre Farms as successful and affordable an egg producer as possible, another antitrust lawsuit was brought against Rose Acre Farms by greedy mega-corporations. This recent case again manipulates and leverages laws intended to protect consumers from the very corporate behemoths using them to benefit themselves over the best interest of the market or consumers.

For context, this whole situation started at the turn of the century, when mega-corporations were strong-arming us into joining the United Egg Producers association. I was confident back then that the decision would come back to bite us, and that's exactly what happened.

No good deed goes unpunished. All the troubles we foresaw when discussing this monumental decision came to pass.

When egg farmers like Rose Acres had joined these regulatory associations at the behest of the big corporations who were their essential customers, the egg farmers necessarily took steps to make their farms compliant with the new regulations. My family knew that the most impactful regulation would be the increased cage space requirements, and that's why we worked so hard to find a way we could comply without destroying our business or unduly burdening consumers.

Unfortunately for the average American, not every farm was as concerned with or capable of mitigating the burden to consumers in the face of those new regulations as Rose Acre Farms was. The price of eggs did go up somewhat, but why? Was it a lack of chickens, or did demand unexpectedly increase? The popularity of low-carb and 'no-carb' diets went through the roof concurrent with these more restrictive regulations, thus the demand for eggs unexpectedly rose beyond forecasted numbers.

Regardless of what market forces caused egg prices to rise somewhat because of greater demand, we are proud of our efforts to avoid being part of that price hike by significantly increasing the number of hens on our own farms.

At that time, we had gone out of our way to mitigate the restriction of production and subsequent consumer price inflation. We incurred massive debts to build extra hen houses on numerous farms so that as we complied with cage space requirements, we could much more than mitigate the subsequent decrease in production in existing houses. Ultimately, we increased our flocks by 6.5 million hens, which meant we were able to continue producing eggs the way we had before we joined and complied with the UEP regulations. This fact alone is why I'm so baffled by this lawsuit against us.

We did what we knew was best for our business, our employees, our hens, and our consumers, even though it was difficult and we just about went broke doing so.

Considering the increased animal rights activism and subsequent public outrage during that time, mega-corporations wanted to virtue signal to their customer base to keep them happy. It was the marketing departments of these mega-corporations that forced us to join a regulatory association and comply with their more restrictive requirements if we wanted to keep their business.

Once we had complied with their demands, it was the legal departments of these same corporations that came after us for breaking antitrust laws because of the effects of complying with the demands previously made by them.

In fact, we were told it was the lawyers from the antitrust case against American farmers that first approached these mega-corporations to drum up clients based on an unethical business model of turning antitrust laws into cash cows for lawyers and large corporations. Our individual contacts in the sales departments of the mega-corporations didn't even know that their corporate headquarters were bringing a lawsuit. It was purely an economic model for the lawyer class to get rich and corporate backers to get power. I'm sure they assumed we would settle, as most are obligated to do when facing years of expensive court battles, but we weren't raised to be chickens when facing pressure.

Even though we had complied with corporate demands and regulatory association rules, that didn't stop the lawsuit from coming. We were accused of price gouging. They alleged that we had conspired to raise egg prices by cutting production, which they claim we did by reducing our flocks under the guise of giving the birds more cage space.

I wish I was surprised by this lawsuit, but we saw it coming from the beginning. I was personally affronted that these mega-corporations would have the gall to accuse us of price gouging when we had bent over backward to comply with their demands and prevent this very thing from happening. As I did when the Animal Liberation Front burned our feed truck, I again wondered if these people even took a moment to consider reality before jumping to action just to send a message.

We worked hard to build new hen houses onto our existing farms so we didn't cause a price rise. We actually significantly increased our flocks and thus increased our production. And we certainly never conspired with other farmers to do any of this as we only joined the UEP because these corporations forced us.

As I had always feared, our motives didn't matter. Incredibly, neither did our actions.

These corporations alleged that we timed the reduction of our flocks for when the hens in certain chicken houses had naturally reached the end of their productive life so that we could make the egg market go up by reducing the bird supply.

It's just a fact of life that as a chicken ages, it no longer can produce an egg a consumer would want to buy. The shell of the egg deteriorates quickly to the point that we can't sell that egg as "Grade A." So, a business decision has to be made for when to sell off that aging flock of chickens.

We are in a business and we have to make enough money to pay our operational costs to feed and maintain the chickens, and to pay our team members. We can't keep unprofitable older flocks if we are to stay in business. Thus, when the egg market is bad and we can't sell the eggs from an older flock anyway, we will at times sell off the entire flock from a particular hen house rather than keeping them on. We are simply making a decision that any common sense farmer would make if they want to remain in business—if you're losing money on something, you try to stop losing money on it.

When flocks have reached the end of their productive years, they are then sold to companies that make other consumer products from them, primarily pet food. Anyone who buys pet food with poultry as an ingredient probably appreciates that the chickens aren't simply discarded at the end of their life. It is merely a responsible business practice to sell those birds to be used for pet food after they are no longer producing eggs for consumers. Is there a law that we have to intentionally lose money by making a bad business decision?

If we followed that logic, we would inevitably conclude that the prices for eggs would skyrocket as our farms would be filled with chickens that can't produce eggs to be sold, thus depriving that capacity for the next flock and cycle of eggs for the consumer. It's completely illogical, yet people will sue for just about anything.

In an attempt to set an outrageous precedent of control, the lawsuit also tried to destroy us by alleging that we sold some of our eggs to customers outside of the United States when egg prices in the United States were low. As it turns out, that's exactly what we did! That's what people with a business in any industry do to continue to make the money necessary to pay their employees, fund their overhead costs, and earn a living. We farmers sell our produce in a manner and on a market that is ultimately beneficial to the longevity of our businesses and farms, often including the global market.

Multi-billion-dollar corporations certainly don't appreciate that farmers have this option, as it contributes to our success and makes us more economically viable long term. They would rather small businesses and farmers be subservient to their own corporate interests for more control over industries, farmers, and consumers.

Interestingly, it's not so much the corporations who seek this control, but those who ultimately control the corporations. Primarily, that's China.

If farms like Rose Acres get shut down, Americans will have to get their eggs from somewhere else. The corporate giants that are crushing American farmers and small businesses have deep financial ties to China, who is ready to swoop in once farms like ours are out of the picture. A prime example is Smithfield Foods, an industrial meat producer, which was purchased by the Hong Kong-based WH Group in 2013 for $4.7 billion. At the time, it was considered "the biggest Chinese takeover" of an American corporation. China is more than eager to control the food supply in America, and therefore control the nation itself.

These mega-corporations want to prevent Rose Acre Farms from being able to sell our eggs on the world market to limit our profits. We would then be unable to pay our employees a fair wage or cover the cost of overhead for the farms. Our business would die, and China would eagerly fill the empty space. Without the competition of farms like Rose Acres, China could achieve a rather sneaky monopoly on the egg market through the efforts of their corporate proxies.

I was baffled by the twisted logic in these allegations of the lawsuit, and terrified of their potential implications. If we farmers can't sell our eggs on the world market but can only accept whatever United States buyers are willing to pay for eggs, then the same would be true of farmers selling their corn, soybeans, beef, and numerous other agricultural products. This would restrict and control the very foundation of our food supply, subjugating consumers to the interests of these massive corporations, which should be a terrifying thought for every American who depends upon a reliable American-owned food production supply.

And what about other non-food American products? We certainly don't claim Ford or General Motors are breaking antitrust laws and ban them from selling American-made cars overseas. That's just good business in a global economy. But the reality is that when corporations have billions of dollars in financial backing from a foreign nation intent on controlling America, they can spend many years and tens of millions of dollars fighting legal battles to destroy any business that is a threat to their control, no matter how illogical these battles may be.

Perhaps the thing that most concerns me about this reality is that I've seen exactly how costly these illogical lawsuits can be, and how long they can drag on. I know from our own lawsuits and my associations with hardworking American farmers and entrepreneurs that most could never survive such lawsuits. These mega-corporations don't even need to be in the right. Like nefarious divorce attorneys, they simply have to outlast their legal opponent as they descend into bankruptcy from the cost of the battle.

Rose Acres has already spent tens of millions of company dollars in legal costs fighting these colossal corporations and their power-hungry financial backers, and this legal fight is far from over. Ironically, that's tens of millions of dollars (and counting) that we can't spend increasing our production or improving our process to be more cost efficient. This means that by suing us over an alleged "conspiracy" to raise the price of eggs, these companies are, in fact, raising the price of eggs themselves and harming the very consumers they pretend to be concerned about.

The elite lawyers of these billion-dollar mega-corporations were able to convince a Chicago jury that we were part of a "conspiracy" to intentionally raise the price of eggs, but we aren't about to bow down to the whims of these corporate monopolies. We know we made the best possible choices not only to survive as a business and keep our employees, but also to protect customers from being harmed.

We are confident this decision by the Chicago jury will be set aside because the facts are on our side. Not only did we significantly increased our egg production after being strongarmed into joining the UEP, but we have faced these same charges before and won!

On June 14th, 2018, a Philadelphia jury returned a verdict completely in favor of Rose Acres. We had been similarly sued by massive national grocery store chains that were seeking more than $1 billion in damages, but the jury found that Rose Acres had not violated any antitrust laws. We knew then and we know now that we did what was right, and we are determined to keep fighting to make sure our case is heard, and that truth prevails.

Just as my dad always feared, free market capitalism is under attack, and the American consumer continues to be the loser. It makes me sick. After working side-by-side with my family as we lived out the American dream, this seems like the worst possible scenario for the nation that I love. It is becoming increasingly unlikely that a young man today could hatch a national egg business out of the back of his pickup truck or raise his children to work the farm and continue to build the family business, as we were blessed to do. If we don't stand and fight to protect these opportunities for future generations, then who will?

I wasn't raised to take the easy way out. I don't give up in the face of inconvenience. I am determined to do what is right even in the face of seemingly invincible opponents, whether it be Mother Nature, greedy corporations, or even the government.

8

A SEED IS PLANTED

LOOKING BACK ON THE many battles that have shaped my life, I realize that most have been, at least in part, fought for others. I tussled with Mother Nature during the blizzard of '77, keeping thousands of chickens alive. I stood beside my dad as we fought to protect American agriculture and free market capitalism from the false promises of marketing orders. And Grandma Otte set a family precedent of fighting legal battles to protect the interests and opportunities of hardworking Americans from the government, a legacy which I would carry on through numerous courtroom clashes to do the same.

Perhaps the most important battle I've ever fought is just beginning.

Most citizens of Indiana did not know that their freedoms had been significantly restricted, specifically their ability to participate in their own governance, which is the foundation of our Constitutional Republic. I certainly didn't know until I tried to participate in what I thought was our participatory democracy and was prevented from doing so by an unconstitutional statute created by the political establishment for their own protection and power.

I wasn't looking for a fight, but I stumbled into one. I quickly realized that this would be a battle not only for myself but for the fundamental rights of democracy afforded to millions of my Indiana neighbors and fellow American citizens in this incredible Constitutional Republic.

I also realized that I had been preparing for this battle my whole life.

As a young man, my mother and father impressed on me important values like commitment, compassion, integrity, and trustworthiness. They showed me how to work hard, care for others, and defend what's right. As I grew, they gave me opportunities to do the same, giving me a deep appreciation for these values and principles. They also showed me how such principles applied in every facet of American society.

This all gave me a deep love for my community and the nation I am so blessed to live in, and as a young man, I closely followed politics. I found that many of my life experiences informed my opinion on important subjects, and I sought out opportunities to be more informed. One of the best opportunities was in my pickup truck.

Over the years, I spent many hours driving to our farms in multiple states to inspect the facilities.

I tried to time my arrival for the very early morning, right when the farms would start to be busy for the day. That way I could walk the hen houses while everyone was on site and get a better feel for how things were running day-to-day.

This timing often had me back in the truck by noon, just in time to turn on the A.M. radio to listen to Rush Limbaugh as I started my drive across the "fruited plain" to the next farm. The first 20 minutes or so of his program were always commercial free, and he would make his most important daily points during that time. I would always try to at least catch that part of his show, but if time permitted while either driving home from a different state or to the next farm, I'd listen to the entire three-hour program.

I spent countless hours over many years considering political issues as I drove and listened to Rush. In hindsight, I'd say that he had more of an impact on my political philosophy than anyone, even Ronald Reagan, of whom I was a big fan. It wasn't just because of his opinions but because of the thought-provoking questions and concerns he raised. He always said it how it really was. He didn't mince words or beat around the bush to placate, and he always fought hard for what he believed. And most importantly, he was always positive in his love of America. That felt right to me.

Going through high school from 1982 to 1985 meant my political mind was influenced by this love of America, as well as all that was encompassed by the cheerful and sunny disposition of Ronald Reagan. I well remember the recession of the early '80s, and that it was brought on by massive spikes in interest rates after rampant Democrat spending under Jimmy Carter.

Our Cort Acre egg farm had a loan on it that had to be paid back at over 18% interest. I was young, but I understood that interest rates at that level were a catastrophe for the American economy. President Reagan brought in some 'tough love' to rein in government spending, cutting taxes and getting the economy back on track after years of Democrat-induced "stagflation."

Back in the day, the Democrat party had traditionally been the party of farmers and the working man and woman. Ronald Reagan loved to point out that he was, in fact, a Democrat. But of course, the Democrat party had left the Farmer and working-class Americans behind. Being a farmer from a family of farmers, I naturally gravitated towards the common-sense side of politics. Early on, I voted in local primary races for people I knew locally or went to church with, and all of whom I knew cared about and understood agriculture and who were pro-business.

I fondly remember accompanying my parents to the polls to cast their ballots back when I was a child. It was a lesson in civics, and Dad never missed an opportunity to teach. Every time we went, I would see Jerry Otte, a distant relative and a man we knew well from the community, working that voting station. When I was old enough to vote myself, Jerry excitedly registered me as a Democrat, and I never thought twice about it because it didn't seem to matter at the time, and the local Jackson County Democrat Party had candidates who were still very pro-business, pro-working class, and pro-farmer that needed support.

However, at the national level, there just weren't any Democrats that I could support. I was, and still am, a firm Reagan Republican. He was unapologetically pro-life, and so am I. His conviction on an issue that was (and still is) controversial stayed with me my entire life. So, I started donating my hard-earned money. I wrote a lot of checks, but only ever to Republican candidates. Despite the sanity that seemed to still exist at the local level, the Democrat Party had long since left common sense behind. Both my heart and my mind were then, and are now, firmly Republican. I wasn't quite old enough to vote for Ronald Reagan, but in 1988 I voted for George Bush when he ran against Michael Dukakis.

In the early '90s, I caught wind that there was a conservative candidate for the House of Representatives out of Indiana. Although he was not running to represent my district, I really liked him and thought he was the kind of representative Hoosiers needed, so I donated $1,000 to David McIntosh. That seemed like a lot of money at the time, but I liked feeling involved in my own governance, as is my right, and perhaps even my duty as an American.

As my FEC filings show, I've only ever donated to conservative Republican candidates, doing so frequently, and I have long and consistently voted exclusively Republican in the fall. For many years, I felt that my votes and donations were sufficient political involvement on my part. Then, in 2016, Senator Ted Cruz ran for the Republican presidential nomination.

I really liked the idea of Ted Cruz as our nation's first Latino president. I was excited about the growth this could mean for our party, and I was impressed by his moral fortitude in the face of his opponents, especially Democrats who labeled him a far-right conservative or disparaged him for breaking from their assumed stereotype that Hispanic Americans are Democrats. He was a man with moral fortitude who didn't back down from a fight despite significant obstacles, and I deeply respected that.

I went with my partner to a Ted Cruz rally in Bloomington, Indiana. For the first time in my life, in front of a small independent grocery store chain on the south side of Bloomington, I saw a presidential candidate, and it was inspiring. I later went to Indianapolis for the announcement of his Vice-Presidential pick, Carla Fiorina. I even got both of their autographs on a campaign placard, which I proudly hang in my campaign office today.

While I enthusiastically voted for Donald Trump as the eventual Republican nominee in the presidential election, I believe this Ted Cruz rally planted a seed I never knew would grow. Perhaps voting and donating simply wasn't enough. Perhaps I needed to do more.

But what more could I, a common-sense Indiana egg farmer, even do? I didn't know. Or perhaps, I wasn't ready to think about it. So, I continued in my duties with the company and in the community, content to be a silent contributor to the system and mostly ignoring that pull to do more.

Then, our nation was turned upside down by the COVID pandemic.

In a bizarrely authoritarian grab for power, our elected government imposed unconstitutional draconian lockdowns and other mandates on supposedly free Americans. Our economy screeched to a halt as schools, churches, and small businesses were forced to close. I was shocked at what was deemed "essential" and what was left to languish under the weight of authoritarianism.

The COVID closures hit our business hard. No, they didn't shutter our hen houses. But they shuttered churches, restaurants, and small stores across the nation. All the Mom-and-Pop shops and diners weren't allowed to be open for business, so they didn't need to buy eggs. Restaurants lost business as people were terrified into isolation, and supposedly scientific mitigation policies made it almost impossible to run food establishments. As universities closed, so did their dining halls. The demand for eggs completely collapsed in these markets.

The drastic drop in demand left us with a huge supply that we couldn't sell. While the egg industry is very cyclical, with a year of profit generally followed by many more years of losses, this was very different. We were hemorrhaging money, but we were utterly determined to make payroll and keep the business running.

We absolutely refused a handout and never took a single penny of government PPP funding. Both Grandma Otte and Dad taught me that independence is one of the most important things a person can possess, and I did not like the idea of our company being beholden to the government, especially due to a crisis their poor judgment and authoritarian tendencies had exacerbated. We weren't about to back down or give in, no matter how hard they tried to crush small businesses.

The only way Rose Acre Farms survived COVID was by selling off a chicken farm and our soybean meal processing plant. Even though some of the decisions we had to make were extremely difficult, we made sure our employees always got paid, we kept our hens healthy, and we were able to continue production for consumers, even though we were losing so much money.

In fact, despite our financial losses during COVID, we continued our longstanding tradition of donating more than 6 million eggs every year to hunger relief organizations that partner with food banks across America. And in 2023, we donated 776,000 dozen, or 9.3 million eggs. Nothing makes us happier than seeing our neighbors and fellow Americans with access to nutritious and fresh protein.

Predictably, political hacks in DC still accused Rose Acres of "price gouging" during COVID. They are the ones who forced these unconstitutional authoritarian policies on our nation, shuttering millions of small businesses, decimating the economy, and destroying the financial futures of millions of hardworking Americans, and we're the ones accused of harming consumers? It's an empty accusation by desperate and guilty politicians, but it's unsurprising considering how hard most of them work to avoid taking personal responsibility. I would argue that many work harder to avoid personal responsibility than anything else in DC. Taking personal responsibility isn't easy, and it requires conviction and integrity, which is largely lacking in our government these days.

As I became increasingly disgusted with the overall state of affairs in America, I frequently had conversations with family and friends about my concerns. In 2021, I stood in our company headquarters with my dear friend and colleague, Gary Bradley. I saw him frequently as he took phone calls at the front desk after losing his eyesight.

Gary has known me most of my life and I trust him as much as I do anyone. He has long been a mentor to many around him and we have had many long conversations on very important matters. During one such conversation, we discussed how the political class was using COVID for their personal gain, and destroying America in the process. Somehow, the idea got thrown around that it was time for me to step up to the plate and run for political office, but I was busy with pressing Rose Acres matters and didn't give it much thought.

But the seed that had been planted in my heart several years before began to stir. I couldn't stop thinking about how the government was using COVID to drastically restrict the rights of Americans. The words of James Carville, frequently quoted by Rush Limbaugh, kept coming back to me— "Never let a good crisis go to waste." The political class clearly wasn't letting this crisis, a unique opportunity to usurp power, go to waste. And America was suffering.

Soon enough, that seed in my heart burst into the sunshine, and I thought that perhaps I really could do more. I could run for office and participate in an extremely substantive way. I could represent the values and interests of the hardworking American people I love so much, and I could protect that which has made this nation great.

In January 2023, I decided to run for the U.S. Senate to represent my beloved state of Indiana and my fellow Hoosiers. Gary stood by my side and gave me the backing that I knew would mean I would be able to actually do it. So, I set about to get things going. I started the process of studying what I needed to have set in place, contacting the local county Republican chairwoman to give her a heads up and see what needed to be done. I even asked her if she had any suggestions for a treasurer for my campaign (perhaps even her) as I knew I would need to get things organized. It was a positive conversation and although I did not know her personally, we had been Facebook friends for some time. She encouraged me to come back to her when I was ready.

In June, I called her to set up a time to talk in person about the next steps. This conversation was when the first alarm bells started ringing in my head that I was doing something 'forbidden' in Indiana. I had just recently heard whispers about something to do with voting in two consecutive party primaries before running for office, but the general consensus seemed to be that it wasn't a big deal and that the county chair could sign off. I didn't think much of it, especially as my very long public financial record showed campaign donations to only Republicans. I was confident that when we sat down for a meeting, the county chair would acknowledge that I had always been a stalwart Republican.

On the phone, we talked cordially about my political positions, opinions, and priorities, and I was sure there was no issue. Then in July, I finally met with her in person to get a letter signed so I could run. I thought she'd be excited to help me make my campaign official. But she was very different during this conversation. In fact, her attitude was the exact opposite of our previous conversation. She seemed upset that I was interested in running and accused me of being a Democrat. I explained to her my rock-ribbed Republican positions and how I had voted for and helped finance Republicans for my entire life.

I was shocked by this bizarre change in attitude. What had happened in these last few months that would cause such a major change in behavior toward me? Then I connected the dots. Back on July 1st, just a few weeks before this meeting, I had filed my federal paperwork to run for the open U.S. Senate seat for the state of Indiana.

It was obvious to me at that moment that the power players behind the scenes, both in Washington and Indianapolis, had reached deep into Jackson County to look for any reason they could to stop me from being on the ballot. As soon as that paperwork had been filed, hit pieces oozing with blatant lies and manipulated facts hit Twitter and fringe media outlets. If they had coordinated with the media to smear me before I was even really a player, of course they could have coordinated with our local political establishment to ice me out. But realizing these things didn't alter my determination. I informed her that I still intended to run.

I reiterated my views and opinions on relevant sociopolitical topics to her and others on the central committee. We all discussed my determination to return decency to society, that pornography in children's spaces is absolutely wrong, that men don't belong in women's sports, and that transgender ideology has no place in classrooms.

I explained how upset I feel seeing our country being run into the ground by politicians who continue to spend money with reckless abandon despite it causing massive inflation that is damaging to everyone. I was adamant that Washington desperately needs candidates like me who have a hard work ethic to get the job done rather than simply leveraging every issue for political gain.

But this all fell on deaf ears. The county chair responded by insisting that I should be running as a Democrat or an Independent. But I'm none of those things. I'm a Republican. A conservative Republican. My positions are nowhere near the modern Democrat party, and to suggest such would be like suggesting Ronald Reagan or Donald Trump should run as Democrats. The only difference might be that they both gave money to the Democrat Party, and I never have. I was rather horrified that she would suggest this.

To my utter astonishment, I was then informed that I wasn't even allowed to run for office as a Republican.

I left the meeting by informing her that I would do whatever it took to get on the ballot as the Republican I am. I simply could not comprehend how this was possible. I thought this was America. I was an upstanding citizen in good legal standing, a meaningful contributor in my community, state, and even the nation, and I wanted to serve. How could I not be allowed to run for office?

I would soon be horrified to discover that I was but one of 81 percent of Hoosiers who are not allowed to run for office because we had been carefully rendered ineligible by sneaky political tricks.

You see, until 2021, the law required that a person who intends to run for office must have previously voted in a primary election of that person's chosen party, a standard which I certainly met. Then, when everyone was distracted by COVID, the Indiana State Legislature changed that law to require a person to have voted in the two consecutive party primaries prior to running for office, limiting who a person can vote for if they want to run for office, and disqualifying someone who didn't meet this new rule. Little fanfare about the change meant little public knowledge of the new rule. In fact, some of the only people who knew about it were the politicians who passed it.

It was passed to protect the politicians who had used the COVID crisis to expand government's power over the will of the people. The politicians knew people would be upset by the usurpation of power, so they worked to change the laws to prevent challengers to their authority and thus avoid accountability.

It was an arcane law which sounded simple on its face, but in practice, it was an exclusionary rule meant to unconstitutionally disenfranchise 81 percent of Hoosier voters from being able to run for office.

Eighty-one percent!

How convenient, then, that the establishment politicians were some of the only Indiana citizens who knew how to ensure their eligibility to run for office, making them some of the only people who could be elected, thus protecting their power. It was an incredibly conniving ploy to eliminate competition in races and maintain political establishment control.

And if the establishment politicians had a potential candidate in mind for a particular office, they could simply install them in the office with this new rule, knowing full well that potential opponents likely wouldn't know and therefore wouldn't be eligible, eliminating them from the ballot before the race even started. The fix was in.

The reality is that our own elected representatives conspired to use an obscure law to manipulate the votes of Indiana citizens by not only influencing but perhaps even hand selecting whose name was allowed to appear on the ballot.

I was truly flabbergasted to think of how many good Hoosiers were being hoodwinked without even knowing it. Citizens dutifully went to the ballot box and cast their vote thinking, like I had for so many years, that they were contributing by making a choice about their governmental representatives. And yet, theirs was only an illusion of choice, as the choice had already been made by the politicians in power before the ballots were even printed. This was truly one of the most egregious examples of undermining democracy within our Constitutional Republic that I had ever heard, and it was completely legal. Was, being the operative word here.

Just as I took but a moment to process the magnitude of the midnight melting mission on the night of the Great Blizzard before I set to work gathering eggs, I processed the shock of this horrifying reality before I got to work righting this outrageous wrong. I had fought many battles before and this one would be no different.

As I walked out of that meeting, I didn't slink back to my truck in defeat. I held my head high, determined to fight for what was right, both for myself and for others. I didn't need to be elected to represent the freedom and best interest of my Hoosier neighbors. I could fight now! The obstacles I had faced with Rose Acres had prepared me for this moment. So, I geared up, ready to take on one of the greatest legal battles to date, fighting to get my name on the ballot to represent the state of Indiana as its next United States Senator.

9

A LOVE LETTER TO HOOSIERS

AS HORRIFIED AS I was with what seemed to be Indiana own 'Incumbent Protection Act' passed during the dark days of COVID for what now seem to be obvious reasons, I wasn't afraid of it. Considering my life experience and tenacity, I figured I was the right guy to fight to protect Hoosiers' right to run for office—a right that had been taken away from 81% of us.

My opponents in this lawsuit were technically the Indiana Secretary of State, the Indiana Election Commission, and the Jackson County Republican Party Chair. Incredibly, these defendants would be represented by lead attorneys who either had positions in the Jim Banks campaign or had donated to him, the career politician who would be my political opponent in the Senate race. It was clear that I was really up against the entire political establishment.

In a historic move, the establishment had already endorsed Banks' candidacy for the Senate, 9 months before the primary and before anyone was even able to file the signature petitions to run for the office. The National Republican Party, the National Republican Senatorial Committee, and the Indiana State Republican Party had all endorsed their stooge. I had filed my federal paperwork to run for the open U.S. Senate seat just a few weeks before, so the elites in Washington worked fast to try to stop me. They had chosen their horse and they weren't going to let anyone else in the race. Heaven forbid someone unsanctioned by the political establishment be allowed to run, because they know I will win!

I'm sure they felt rather secure in their power with this sneaky legal statute meant to protect political insiders and help them prevent candidates they cannot control. But they clearly didn't know me. I wasn't about to back down from a fight against a goliath. I've fought such battles plenty of times, and I'm still standing.

I quickly realized what it meant to be up against the political establishment. I was rather disappointed to hear that David McIntosh, the conservative candidate and worthy Hoosier representative to whom I had donated thousands of dollars to so many years ago, was now the chairman for a major PAC called Club for Growth, funded primarily by out-of-state billionaires, according to financial records.

After asking me for money in the 1990s and calling me a "good Republican" for being willing to donate and help fight together for our shared concern for a strong conservative agenda, the word around the state these days is that McIntosh is ready to throw his political weight and millions of PAC dollars in with the establishment to defeat me in a run against Banks.

This support for Banks is ironic considering that his record is falsely conservative, with lots of 'show' votes for bills supporting conservative causes that have little realistic chance of being signed into law. But when the votes really matter, he fails to show up or he votes the party establishment line, contradicting the will and best interest of the American people. And yet, he is the establishment's pick.

I guess I shouldn't be surprised by any of this. They are happy to stroke our ego and call us "good Republicans" when they are asking us for more money, but as soon as we try to take our lives and well-being into our own hands by participating in our own government, they turn on us. They don't actually want us to have a say. They just want our money.

The political establishment wants the people to unwittingly elect the candidates they've already chosen to do the bidding of the corporate and political machines. Everyone else must be defeated.

Jim Banks has a pathetic record of voting the exact opposite of what he pretends to stand for when he visits Indiana, so they are scared of anyone challenging him. They know I will defeat Jim Banks, the establishment's clear favorite. I leapt into action immediately after filing the necessary paperwork to run. But to win, I'd first have to get on the ballot. And that was being blocked by this darkly conspiratorial law. I immediately hired a dynamite attorney. I like to think of Michelle Harter as the Erin Brockovich of Indiana election law, and the first thing she had to do was get me through the depositions.

I spent many frustrating hours sitting across the table from the attorneys for the defense. As I sat in the hot seat, they took their sweet time asking me extremely personal and often vulgar questions about myself and my family. I figured it was an attempt to goad me into reacting in a way that might damage my case. Despite the wholly uncomfortable and inappropriate interrogation, I was confident that I was on the right side of this issue, and if this was how I needed to fight for what I knew was right, then I'd gladly endure the ridiculous and inappropriate questioning.

I gritted my teeth and put on a pleasant face as I answered everything, including their crass questions. I have nothing to hide so I answered straightforwardly. As it turned out, though, none of those awful questions mattered one bit for the lawsuit. It was purely a fishing expedition by the Banks campaign-related attorney, probably to take the opportunity provided by the deposition to dig up dirt they could use to smear me once they had to campaign against me.

One of their ridiculous lines of questioning was about where I lived. For two hours, the lawyers hounded me about the location of my home, asking dozens of slightly changed versions of the same question. My house is in the woods, seemingly in the middle of nowhere, and I love it that way. I love rural Indiana. Where I live doesn't even have mail service, so I've always used my mom's house as my address for receiving mail, as it is less than a mile away as the crow flies. This detail led to hours of pointless questioning.

Lots of rural Hoosiers live in similar circumstances, so this is by no means unheard-of, and there are election laws dealing specifically with this circumstance. But the Jim Banks campaign (even though Jim Banks himself has a million-dollar home in Virginia) and his political establishment allies were clearly looking for anything they could use to defeat me, no matter how silly or insignificant. They realized that the only chance their preferred candidate has of walking onto the U.S. Senate floor is if he is forced on Hoosier voters whether they like him or not.

The whole situation was disheartening for someone who loves Indiana as much as I do. Here we had state-funded lawyers in the camp of my would-be political opponent trying to find any exclusionary technicality or dig up unflattering information on me, ultimately on the taxpayer's dime. I suspect the state assumes that if someone were to slip through the sneaky law that excludes 81% of Hoosiers from running for office, then subjecting citizens to this kind of treatment would intimidate them into reconsidering. Does that sound like a government for and by the people?

Far from intimidating me, embarking on this journey has only given me nerves of steel and has strengthened my resolve. It has cemented my knowledge that the establishment only cares about their power. Nothing else matters to them. Nothing. Certainly not voters. If they're willing to go to such great lengths to prevent me from running, they must be incredibly nervous about what I would do to their reign of power and control in Washington and in the United States Senate. In fact, I think that the slimy tactics by the state will tip the scales in my favor in this United States Senate race.

The stakes are too high.

Good Americans are sick to death of the establishment and the state protecting their own, ensuring their goons and stooges become the only candidates to choose from. This circle of self-perpetuating power over the people cannot continue. My lawsuit would expose the entire scheme and challenge the unconstitutional legal statute.

On November 1, 2023, the day of the hearing that also served as a trial on the merits, my sister, bus driver (Mike Wilson, who previously worked with me at Rose Acres), and I loaded into the campaign bus and headed to the courthouse. There wasn't really a campaign yet, since I was still fighting to even be allowed on the ballot, but I was already representing the people of Indiana and I wanted everyone to see that there is someone advocating for their rights and freedom. The American flag was already proudly emblazoned on each side of the bus. This was a fight for American rights. This whole legal battle was just a frustratingly necessary chore before my actual campaign.

We met Michelle at the brand new and very modern courthouse. It was just me fighting this political machine, so our table in the courtroom only had the two of us. I had worn my most beloved tie— vintage 1976 with the American flag and the numbers 1776 weaved into the design. Our founding fathers set forth the constitution to protect the citizens against the power of the state, and that was exactly what I was there to fight to continue.

On the other side of the courtroom were seated four lawyers, but no named defendants. Even the county chair, with whom I had personally dealt several months before, was a no-show. This was potentially a landmark case and no one bothered to show up for their side.

It spoke volumes that only the hired guns showed up to try to keep me off the ballot. No one else was willing to stand publicly for it. I suspect they knew what they were doing was wrong and they knew it went against the democratic principles that have made America the freest nation in the world. They were essentially advocating for "taxation without representation" by making taxpayers fund the primary process, but not allowing 81% of Hoosiers to participate! An authoritarian government trying to make the United States Senate into an unrepresentative House of Lords chosen by the establishment elite is exactly what the Founding Fathers fought to prevent, and what the 17th Amendment to the United States Constitution clearly forbids.

But they were all doing a job for the establishment, and apparently no one was brave enough to challenge that. Except for me.

Michelle, who teaches a business law class, had invited all her students to attend the hearing and see what it looks like when government entities get too big for their britches and forget that they serve, not control, the people. She wanted them to be inspired to protect and defend constitutional liberties and American freedom, not use our laws to undermine them.

The hearing itself lasted about three hours but my heart was bursting with pride for every second of it. I've sat through many trials and court proceedings, waiting with bated breath to hear how my family's business would be impacted. This one was different. I wasn't pleading a case about regulations regarding chickens; I was pleading a case for the rights and liberties of millions of Hoosiers.

Sure, other trials certainly dealt with important issues like free markets and the American economy, but this one just seemed to strike more at the heart of fundamental American freedom. In that moment, I felt like I was all that stood between an increasingly authoritarian political machine and the good and hardworking Indiana citizens. We simply had to win.

Michelle delivered an extremely detailed argument regarding how the legal statute requiring potential candidates to vote in the two consecutive previous party primaries violated the state and federal constitutions by denying Hoosiers the ability to freely associate with the party of their choosing, as well as by treating Hoosiers differently based on circumstances outside their control like where they live, who their party chair is, their age, etc.

She also explained how the statute was similar to a different statute that was previously struck down for being too broad, and how the statute violates the 17th Amendment which gives the people, not the state legislature, the power to choose Senators. By using their own restrictive and quietly passed law, the legislature was choosing Senators by hand-picking who even had the opportunity to be elected. Hers was fundamentally an argument for the citizens.

The arguments by the lawyers in defense of the political establishment machine were mostly what you'd expect—not for the citizens. Essentially, the state had to prove how denying citizens the right to run for office served the American people, and specifically the state of Indiana. Considering how anti-American that is, I can hardly believe we had to sit through all that. But there we were. I'll never forget the disgust and incredulity that permeated the courtroom when they argued that the political parties had the right to exclude any candidate they wanted. They prefer the people only have the illusion of choice, not an actual choice.

Overall, the judge seemed pleased with the quality of the oral arguments, remarking that they were some of the best he had ever heard in his time on the bench. I found the whole proceeding to be interesting, especially from the perspective of the plaintiff. But once these arguments were over, we had to simply wait for the judge's decision. After a life of constant hard work, I'm more of an action kind of guy, so this was a frustrating few weeks. I spent the entire time on my campaign bus continuing to tour the state of Indiana, talking to voters, and getting signatures for my ballot access petitions. When I started my campaign in August, I announced that I would visit all 92 counties in Indiana before the end of the year, and I have now accomplished that goal.

The whole process became worth it when the judge handed down his decision granting an injunction. His masterful decision reads like a love letter to Hoosiers.

As is customary in such hearings, Michelle had drafted and submitted a powerful draft decision in our favor, which the judge largely adopted, but also made striking additions. Every single one of the 27 pages contains powerful statements regarding the rights and freedoms we are blessed to enjoy in this nation and in the state of Indiana, and I cherish every word on every page.

The decision starts by reiterating a statement by Indiana Governor Eric Holcomb's in a 2020 speech titled, "True Equality and Equity leads to Opportunity for All." He was right when he said that "over our country's long history, inequity and exclusion have actually been engrained in many of our institutions, systems and structures—often unknowingly.

And while we've made progress, we haven't rooted it out fast enough." This case was fundamentally about inequity and exclusion within American political institutions, systems, and structures.

This 2021 law was passed without fanfare, thus the majority of Hoosiers never heard of it. I certainly didn't. It wasn't intended to serve or protect the people. It was passed with the aim to give career politicians a mammoth leg-up over any competition. It effectively banned average citizens from running for office unless they met legal thresholds that were both arbitrary and capricious.

If you were an insider and knew the secret handshake, so to speak, then you were allowed to run. If you were not an insider but had bought off the right people to be in the know, then you were allowed to run. The reality is that no one else is really wanted by the political establishment, so they made it so they probably wouldn't be allowed to run anyway.

I didn't pay anyone off and I didn't know the 'secret handshake' (voting in two previous consecutive party primaries), so, despite always voting for Republicans in every Presidential election of my entire life, the political establishment knew I wasn't who they wanted running for office. And that's not how our government is supposed to be. It's a blatant abuse of power.

One of the most salient parts of the court's order granting my injunction and striking down the unconstitutional statute spoke directly to this abuse by the state:

"When the immense power of the state is turned toward and upon its citizens in such a way that it imperils a sacred and cherished right of those same citizens, the state's actions must be for an articulated compelling and pressing reason, and it must be exercised in the most transparent and least restrictive and least intrusive ways possible. The 2021 amendment to I.C. § 3-8-2-7(a)(4)

fails in this regard. It unduly burdens Hoosiers' long-recognized right to freely associate with the political party of one's choosing and to cast one's vote effectively."

The judge recognized the undue burden this sneaky legal requirement placed on upstanding and civic-minded Hoosiers. He reiterated in his decision that "the purpose of election laws is to protect the will of the voter and prevent disenfranchisement."

"Before turning to the constitutionality of the statute, it is helpful to recognize what the Indiana Supreme Court aptly stated long ago about the very purpose of all election laws:

*The purpose of all election laws is to secure a free and honest expression of the voter's will. Statutes controlling the activities of political parties, party conventions, and primaries, and providing for the manner in which the names of candidates may be put upon the ballots, have for their only purpose the orderly submission of the names of candidates for office to the electors to the end that the electors may know who are candidates and have a free opportunity to vote for their choice, and that the ballots may not be incumbered by the names of those who have no substantial support. . . **The purpose of the law and the efforts of the court are to secure to the elector an opportunity to freely and fairly cast his ballot, and to uphold the will of the electorate and prevent disfranchisement."***

Marion Superior Court Judge Patrick Dietrick's decision continued on to quote one of the greatest men in our nation's history—Abraham Lincoln:

"As another Hoosier raised lawyer was once heard to remark: "Elections belong to the people. It's their decision." Six Months at The White House with Abraham Lincoln: The Story of a Picture by F. B. Carpenter (Francis Bicknell Carpenter), Ch. 68, p. 275. It is with this purpose in mind that the court renders its decision."

That really is the crux of it—elections belong to the people. Not to the political establishment. The people should have their say because it's their decision. But if the political establishment is carefully manipulating legal statutes to help them dictate who is allowed to have a vote cast for them, how is that the people's decision?

Interestingly, this is not the first time this unconstitutional statute has been challenged. In 2022, two other candidates challenged it on similar legal grounds, after they were removed from the ballot. They lost their cases and the appellate courts refused to decide the issues on the merits because the election had passed, and so the appellate courts deemed the matters moot.

But my case was brought prior to the election. This time, the defendants tried to say that the case had been brought too soon (rather than too late like the other cases), but luckily for Hoosier voters, the judge did not buy that argument.

In fact, the judge didn't seem to be buying much of what the political establishment was trying to sell, and the court ultimately struck down the statute as unconstitutional on five separate legal bases, finding that it violated both the United States federal and Indiana state constitutions.

Regarding the federal constitution, the court found that the statute violates Hoosiers' rights to freely associate with the party of their choosing, that the statute was overly broad and vague, and that the statute violates the 17th Amendment regarding who elect Senators.

When it comes to the Indiana state constitution, the court found that the statute discriminates against candidates based on characteristics that have nothing to do with the candidate—who their party chair is and when they ran for office (now versus in the past when the statute was less restrictive).

Additionally, it was found to discriminate against citizens who are younger or who moved to Indiana from out of state.

The judge also decided that this statute added to what the Indiana constitution required of citizens to be able to run for office, and thus was an inappropriate constitutional amendment that did not go through the proper constitutional amendment process. On top of that, he decided that the party chair, Amanda Lowery, misapplied the unconstitutional statute to me in numerous ways. But that doesn't surprise me at all considering the lengths to which they seemed willing to go to prevent me from having the opportunity to be elected.

In the end, this decision to grant an injunction officially struck down this statute as unconstitutional and means that it cannot be enforced against myself or any other Hoosier, unless a higher court lifts this injunction.

I will forever remember the moment I heard about this landmark decision to protect freedom and empower citizens to participate in government. It was Thursday, December 7th, a day that already lives in infamy after Pearl Harbor was bombed, beginning our involvement in World War Two. As American freedom was defended on that day those many years ago, it was now being defended in another way—in a courtroom. On that historic afternoon, I was driving in my campaign bus when I got a text message from my campaign saying that the judge had released his decision and that I had won!

My heart was pounding as I immediately called Michelle to confirm, and she informed me that the judge had indeed ruled in my favor, and in the favor of 81% of Hoosiers who had been unconstitutionally disenfranchised. It was a landmark decision, soon called the most important legal decision in Indiana of this century. I had fought and won back the rights of Hoosiers!

I was filled with an overwhelming sense of relief. This was exactly what I was fighting for—to protect all Hoosiers from being manipulated and oppressed by a powerful political establishment that seeks to protect its own and control the people. Although this case was ruled in my favor, it wasn't really about me. It was about being entirely committed to a fight for what was right, representing the best interest of my fellow Hoosiers, and standing up to the establishment.

Now that I had proven my commitment to representing hardworking Hoosiers and fighting for the freedoms of this great nation, I was ready to take the fight to Washington DC. This landmark win was only the first victory in a battle to protect the American people from powerful entities intent on quietly seizing control and manipulating the masses. For me, the fight had just begun.

10

MAKE AMERICA DECENT AGAIN

AS THE SECOND YOUNGEST in the family, I was pretty low in the pecking order, and I wasn't handed success. I learned quickly to step up to the plate, work hard for what I wanted to achieve, and fight for what I knew was right. That's the kind of man I was raised to be and that's what we are lacking in our government.

My father modeled incredible leadership skills and an outstanding work ethic through my youth. My mother also demonstrated keen financial sense and equal commitment and drive. But that doesn't mean things were easy. In fact, they have almost always been hard.

Despite growing up in a business that continued to expand into a rather large nationwide operation, we lived hand to mouth, as everything was put back into the business and used to keep our family financially independent. In the 70s, we lived as any farm family in Indiana would have lived—a house with no air conditioning, a single bathroom for all nine of us, and a single small black and white TV. Entertainment was hands-on and outdoors, often with some productive angle because our time had to be used carefully.

On a chicken farm, there are no days off. Eggs are laid seven days a week, 365 days a year, (including holidays like Christmas and Thanksgiving), so that's when we would work. We would wake up early to make the most of the day and deal with problems as they arose instead of putting them off for someone else to deal with later. Farmers who kick the can down the road aren't farmers for long.

Running a business every single day unsurprisingly leads to everyday issues, some larger than others. In fact, we had a phone line dedicated entirely to dealing with potential problems. Like most houses, we had a party line that we shared with neighbors and used for everyday phone calls. We were also lucky enough to have a dedicated business line that was exclusively used by Mom and Dad. They couldn't have neighbors accidentally cutting into an important business call. But the third line was an emergency line wired directly into Mom and Dad's bedroom from the Jen Acre egg farm.

On occasion, that emergency phone would ring, perking our ears and bringing us all to attention, as it was never good news. Sometimes, the call notified us of something my father or mother could deal with alone or at least make the necessary arrangements to solve the issue. But that wasn't the case one day in 1972.

We were already facing issues that day before the phone rang. The power was out, meaning the ventilation fans were down. Without them, our chickens were as good as dead. Mom and dad had prepared for this issue, as it wasn't the first time we lost power. With the backup generators up and running, the problem was solved.

That's what made hearing the emergency phone that much more dreadful. We had already dealt with the power outage problem; what more could it be?

As soon as we saw the panicked expression on Mom and Dad's faces, we knew it was bad, and she quickly relayed the message to the rest of us. Jen Acres was burning!

One of the generators caught fire, sparking an inferno that quickly engulfed some of the chicken houses and knocked out the back-up power to the hen houses. As soon as that emergency line rang, everyone in the family sprang into action. Just like the Great Blizzard, it was all-hands-on-deck. There was no option to leave this problem for someone else to deal with.

I was too young to be much help in the face of the massive blaze, but I watched from the sidelines, awestruck, as all the older family members frantically did what they could to save the sweltering chickens, including opening "knock out" doors to provide ventilation to nearby chicken houses that were growing hotter by the minute. With multiple large chicken houses and multiple doors on each that needed to be knocked out, it was a physically demanding, dangerous, and time-sensitive job, especially as the fire raged nearby, threatening to jump to other structures.

I'll never forget standing there, small and helpless. Smoke and flames began to engulf the farm in front of me, higher than I could even see. My older siblings stood bouncing on the balls of their feet, poised and desperate to race into the fire and knock out one of those doors once allowed.

After hours fighting the blaze, we were devastated to lose two chicken houses and the entire egg grading and processing building. Thankfully, my family took action when they did, or it could have been far worse. That day, I gained a new appreciation for my family's dedication to preparedness with that emergency phone line, as well as a greater understanding of how important it is to put out fires as they arise (whether real or metaphorical), rather than leaving them for others to take care of.

The experience lit a fire under me, showing me that life on the egg farm was more than a fulltime job. If we weren't constantly working to monitor and improve operations, as well as addressing problems immediately, then arising issues would compound and get so out of control that they would become extremely difficult to fix, likely destroying our company. This is the reality in any business, really.

Perhaps the only organization in which this doesn't apply is government.

Somehow, Congress ambles in on a Tuesday afternoon, squabbles about how much more money should be tossed at failing initiatives or programs, makes excuses for the problems that continue to be ignored, then ambles back home two days later.

Occasionally, they come together long enough to sign a bill, spending trillions of dollars our country does not have on initiatives that hardworking Americans do not need or want. As problems inevitably arise, they figure the next guy will deal with it. Meanwhile these ineffective programs and initiatives with limited oversight either fail to attain their objective or, quite often, make things worse.

Even as taxpayers are being forced to shoulder the social and financial burden of a massive immigration crisis, Congress and our other elected officials fail to put a stop to it. Instead, they funnel billions of taxpayer dollars to secure the borders of foreign nations, then spend even more money to deal with the symptoms of the immigration crisis like housing, relocating, and educating the illegal immigrants being allowed into our nation. Somehow, our government representatives don't realize that this actually makes the inflation, crime, and immigration issues worse.

I can't imagine how much more could be accomplished for the American people if our elected representatives showed up ready to work hard every single day, monitoring or improving operations and addressing problems immediately and directly. Actually, I think I can imagine! Like I said before, farmers who don't work hard aren't farmers for long because natural selection eliminates them. So why isn't it the same in government?

The answer is exactly why I went to court—the political establishment protects its own at the expense of hardworking Americans.

This is one of the main reasons I decided to run for office at the beginning of 2023. Christmas is usually a joyful time of year, but during the Christmas season of 2022, my mind was in turmoil. Social media companies had been conspiring with government entities to clamp down on free speech while the news media had also been conspiring with government entities to carefully curate information. I, along with many other Americans, didn't know what was true.

Freedom of speech in the United States had reached an impressive low.

When Elon Musk purchased Twitter, things started to change. As the year came to a close, I was heartened to see renewed enthusiasm for free and open expression of ideas. After so much draconian censorship by the elites within our society and government, it felt validating to see the evidence of this collusion to censor, and I hoped this evidence would lead to some accountability, for the good of all Americans on all sides of all issues.

I despise identity politics. I strongly believe in Martin Luther King, Jr's sentiment that we should be judged by the content of our character and not the color of our skin (or the emojis and imagined pronouns in our bio). I am first and foremost an American and see others as such. We are all equal under the law. None of us has any rights over any other citizen and no one should be treated differently in an effort to 'make up for' past wrongs. But the Left has twisted the idea of 'equal rights for all' into one of 'special rights for some,' elevating them within society purely to divide us and serve the interest of identity politics.

Working in numerous states across the nation, I have come to know and love people of many walks of life, skin colors, and backgrounds. I have seen their hard work and determination to achieve their goals, and I respect their tenacity. Every day, industrious Americans prove themselves by their merit and create their own success in this land of freedom and opportunity. That's what my dad did when he started Dave's Produce out of a pickup truck in rural Indiana, and that's what I'm fighting to protect as partisan activists seek to tear down the values and principles that are the foundation of this nation.

One of these fundamental values is merit. I firmly believe that winners should be chosen by merit, not activist agendas and certainly not by the government. The sad reality is that many people in government are folks who couldn't hack it in the private sector. There are a lot of 'empty suits' there—the kind of people who like to have meetings about having meetings, but never really get anything done. As with farming, natural selection takes care of the companies that have too many empty suits.

Unfortunately, when those empty suits get into government, they enjoy the protection of the establishment from being removed by natural selection. With this security, they become career politicians with no accountability other than the ballot box. And my case proves that even the ballot can be manipulated to protect these career 'empty suit' politicians from being held accountable. If it's happening in Jackson County, Indiana, you can be sure it's happening across the country.

With a government full of inept and power-hungry career politicians, it's not just egg farmers that have suffered. It's hardworking Americans who pay the price for the system that helps them avoid accountability. How many Americans lost their jobs, businesses, or even loved ones as a result of the irresponsible and agenda-focused COVID response? And have we seen any real accountability for the implementation of the policies that were known to be illogical, unscientific, and ultimately damaging?

Even the Republican Party, which purports to be the party of small government and fiscal responsibility, is part of this system. They cast 'show votes' to virtue signal their supposed work for the American people but continue to elect leadership that works with Democrats to grow government, usurp power, and undermine American values, rendering those votes meaningless for everyday Americans. They accomplish nothing, sometimes even making things worse, and still get off scot-free as they are perpetually protected by a system that prioritizes government power over the will and interest of the people.

Despite the best efforts of conniving powerful entities and radical activists in this nation, I have seen that Americans are fundamentally decent. Our representatives in government should reflect that decency and fight to preserve it, not throw in with those who seek to destroy it, of whom there are many. Terrifyingly, our children are largely the target of their efforts, as they know where the American future lies. If they can corrupt our children, they can corrupt the nation.

Classrooms are being infiltrated by radical activism and are quickly becoming epicenters of indoctrination, discouraging the concepts of unity, merit, and hard work. Instead of effectively educating our youth and promoting positive values for social and individual success, schools condemn these values as racist and bigoted and focus on identity, dividing by race and gender.

Many schools have done away with the morning Pledge of Allegiance, and American flags have given way to all manner of social agenda flags. Even the seemingly virtuous "no child left behind" policy has devolved into "every child moves on whether they're ready to or not because it might hurt someone's feelings if they don't." This only sets our children up for failure when they are faced with new concepts for which they aren't prepared because they were allowed to move on despite their inadequacies. And you wouldn't believe the number of American youths who can't even read or find our country on a world map.

Children are our future, and we are doing them a disservice by giving them free passes and dumbing down their education.

Instead of teaching reading, writing, and math, activists in education and society pump our children's minds with radical ideology and filth in a grotesque attack on their right to innocence. Drag queen shows are promoted as "family friendly" and sexual content is weaved into every facet of children's entertainment and other content. When decent parents object and seek to protect their children from this filth, activists scream about "book banning" and "bigotry," vilifying good parents for daring to object.

But I'm willing to loudly object, and I'm not afraid to be vilified for standing up for what is right. I was raised to be morally decent. Having known many truly incredible women, including my mother who took me to Sunday school before church every week, I view the drag queen trend to be extremely degrading to real women. The entire genre is a cartoonish and negative portrayal of women as derisive and outrageous sex objects. It's blackface, but for gender.

Oddly, drag has become a politically 'safe' form of blackface. Publicly sexualizing, degrading, and stereotyping women has become widely accepted as a perverse form of entertainment, just as blackface once was. Just because something is widely accepted doesn't mean it's right. The only reason any adult, whether gay or straight, would want to perform (and it is a performance) in a sexualized manner in front of children is to satisfy their own sexual desires. That's not decency. It's degrading and morally repugnant.

It's also part of a movement intended to sow confusion. In a world where truth is censored and so-called "experts" say whatever the highest bidder demands, one constant reality is that men are human beings born with the sexual organs associated with males and women are human beings born with the sexual organs associated with females. Put bluntly, men are men and women are women.

I was truly flabbergasted when a Supreme Court nominee said that she was unable to define the word "woman." In a world filled with phenomenal women who have changed the course of history in so many ways, herself included, how incredibly diminutive to pretend like there is ambiguity in womanhood. How can she possibly adjudicate the law fairly when she refuses to acknowledge one of the most fundamental human truths?

In the name of inclusion, women have been forced out of female spaces. Biological men who were mediocre in male competition are dominating women's sports, forcing them out of scholarships, sponsorships, prize money, and athletic placement, and increasingly injuring their female competitors. After so many years fighting for women's rights and female equality, this movement is once again placing women below men in society.

Even the concept of equality has been hijacked by extremist movements like the radical gender ideology community, which changes what 'rights' are as fast as they change the LGBTQIA+ acronym of the moment. All of a sudden, we're told that while everyone is 'equal,' some people are more equal than others. At least, they're more preferred among the equal. I've simply never lived like this, treating certain people better or simply differently than others.

As I've said before, I don't believe in identity politics. In this day and age, it frankly doesn't matter to people who my spouse or partner is. What matters is what we contribute with our minds and our hands. I don't profess to have any rights over anyone else. I don't expect preferential treatment or special consideration simply because I can be ascribed to a particular demographic. Nor do I feel that it would be appropriate to force my choices on others who may choose differently.

I have always been dedicated to contributing positively to our community and I only want equal rights under the law, and to be treated with equal dignity, respect, and consideration as any hardworking and law-abiding citizen deserves. And I've done my best to exemplify this in my own life.

For years, I traveled to numerous farms in many states, spending time with as many employees in every job I could. I was happy to work alongside every one of them, jumping in if ever there was something they needed help with, and seeking help from them when I needed it. I came to know many of them, hearing about their lives and families, as well as their struggles and dreams. Their personal identity or their position in the company didn't matter. Not everyone was the same and not every job was the same, but every person was treated with equal dignity and respect and given equal opportunity for growth and success.

That is perhaps the greatest privilege we enjoy in America—the freedom of equal opportunity and prosperity. Unfortunately, that freedom is under attack as the American economy is burning down faster than our Jen Acres chicken houses. The future of our nation may depend on electing hardworking and dedicated people who have the understanding and experience to get our economy back on track, and who aren't afraid to extinguish the flames of radical ideology before all that's left of our society is politically correct ash and dust.

11

A LAND OF OPPORTUNITY
AND PROSPERITY

AMERICA IS KNOWN AROUND the world for her freedoms—
freedom to worship, freedom to speak, and freedom to pursue
happiness. Perhaps equally appreciated in this nation is the
freedom to enjoy limitless opportunities and attain prosperity, contingent on our willingness to put forth the effort
to achieve our dreams. Just as my parents taught me, ours is a
land of unlimited possibilities.

At least, it has been. Unfortunately for hardworking
Americans and future generations, the scope of our possibilities is fast shrinking as the economy circles the drain. The
Senate and House of Representatives are full of people who
could barely earn a paycheck, much less have experience with
signing the front of one. And yet, they are somehow trusted
to handle hundreds of billions of taxpayer dollars. Mishandle,
really. That's why we're facing historically high inflation, the
subsequent devaluation of the dollar, and increased cost of
living for every taxpayer.

For as long as I can remember, I've despised taxation
as being used as legal theft. Perhaps it started when I heard
about Grandma Otte fighting the IRS to keep her farm intact.
Or perhaps it was growing up working hard every day for
every penny our family earned and needed in order to survive.
Either way, I was already voicing my opinion on the matter
before I could even drive.

Back when I was about 15 years old, I wrote a letter to read to the group at a Saturday Night Meeting. I'd written many before, but this one was addressed to then-United States Congressman Lee Hamilton. In that letter, I made a statement with which I still agree to this day— "Taxes are the drugs that politicians are addicted to."

Even back then, I knew that it's easy for these politicians to spend money that isn't theirs. They didn't work hard every day for it, and they won't miss it when they try to make payroll or head to the grocery store. All they have to do is show up for a day or two and argue about how to mishandle billions of other peoples' dollars on activist agendas or failing programs.

How much official time and taxpayer money do our politicians spend on such agendas and programs, like developing the now massive field of "diversity, equity, and inclusion" (DEI), one of the largest growth industries in corporate America? I remember hearing jokes about meaningless college degrees like "underwater basket weaving" while I was encouraged to get a meaningful education. Now, it's no joke, as "gender studies" and "DEI" have become common majors.

In a true free market, such ridiculous fields of study would be eliminated by natural selection and taxpayer money wouldn't be wasted on such destructive ideologies. They make no real contribution to society, instead draining resources that are desperately needed to deal with real-world issues facing hardworking Americans. But students of "gender studies" and "DEI" realized there were no jobs associated with such fields of study unless they were imposed. And our government has agreed to impose them.

I can't help but think of Bud Light as a prime example of how free markets can facilitate natural selection when left to their own devices. Bud Light's brand management has been increasingly infected by destructive radical activism.

Eventually, they were so far gone that they thought it was a good idea to put a transgender social media influencer and drag queen on the can of a beverage long enjoyed by millions of hardworking and rational-minded Americans.

The once beloved American brand experienced a subsequent loss of market share and lower sales. The American people realized that the company cared more about promoting and celebrating radical gender ideology than creating an exceptional product for consumers. In a free market, consumers voted with their pocketbooks when they stopped buying Bud Light products, telling the company that they didn't appreciate their radical activism and forcing them to change course.

But in government, the politicians doing the same thing as Bud Light are protected by the establishment from the consequences of a free market. They continue to implement these expensive and destructive agendas and programs with the confidence that they will never be held accountable in the way Bud Light was.

Put bluntly, it's nothing but an added expense to create a "solution" for a problem that doesn't exist. The free market could take care of this issue and save the American taxpayers millions in the form of government overspending, but the government won't allow that, preferring to spend money we don't have on agendas and programs we don't need or want, destroying the economy, devaluing the dollar, and driving up national debt.

Our national debt was $160,000 per taxpayer just over eight years ago. Now, it's $260,000 per taxpayer, and it's going up weekly at an alarming rate. This debt is driving interest rates up and lowering the standard of living for working class Americans. Our elected representatives don't seem to care. They spend money that isn't theirs with reckless abandon, secure in the knowledge that they will be protected by the political establishment from taking responsibility for their choices.

How many of them really know what it's like for the hardworking citizens shouldering the burden of their financial ineptitude and poor judgment? Have they gone grocery shopping recently and seen how little our money buys these days? I sure have!

On May 5th, 2023, I was in Arizona to give a speech at the ground-breaking ceremony of our newest two million-hen cage-free farm. I had already been getting my "hens" in a row to run for Senate when an experience that day strengthened my resolve. As I would be speaking at the ceremony, I decided to head to the local grocery store to check the price of eggs so I could accurately report it in my speech.

Egg prices in the stores around there were reasonable for what we call "commodity" eggs, but I saw some listed as costing more than nine dollars a dozen. These were "boutique" blue and brown pasture raised eggs, but standard Grade A Large white chicken eggs were reasonably priced. For reference, the midwestern retail price through most of 2023 was under $2.00/dozen, about one third the price of a fancy coffee at Starbucks. This is thanks in part to the efficiency efforts of farms like Rose Acres.

As I left the shelves of refrigerated eggs, I overheard one of the most tragic conversations I can remember in recent years. An elderly couple stood in the snack aisle with a cart holding just a few items. The wife asked her husband to "go grab your favorite chips." I didn't see which brand, but I saw him look at the price and remark, "They cost too much. I'll do without them this week. Maybe next week we can get some."

My heart sank as I heard this. I could imagine them feeling desperate about how little they could afford despite having worked their whole lives to be able to retire and enjoy a weekly bag of their favorite potato chips. I thought of the many lifelong Rose Acres employees who we love like family. As much as we love them, we're always happy to see them able to retire. Unfortunately, we now see some of these beloved employees forced out of retirement as inflation has wiped out the savings they thought would sustain them for years.

As I looked around me, I saw numerous other elderly couples, parents with children, and young adults who were all certainly in the same situation—pinching pennies because their pennies aren't worth what they used to be. They grab a package of cookies, relieved to see that the price hasn't changed much, but fail to notice that while it may cost the same, the package now holds a lot fewer cookies it used to.

It's not just potato chips and cookies that cost more these days. Inflation has hit every aspect of American life. Young families are realizing that they can no longer afford the home they have been saving for. These days, their money only buys half the house it would have just a few years ago. Couples are changing their weekly dinner date to a monthly one, as the meal bill continues to climb. All the while, we watch as our savings accounts are wiped away by inflation.

Not only are our savings prematurely depleted, but elderly couples like the one I overheard in that store also see their pensions and social security threatened. After decades of paying into a committed retirement benefit that they have earned, they are being denied the fruits of their labor to pay the cost of the government's fiscal irresponsibility. Meanwhile, career politicians are promised fat government pensions with guaranteed inflation adjustments for life, all on the taxpayer dime.

What's more, some elected representatives are even fighting to raise the retirement age, relegating citizens to working almost until they die. How convenient for the politicians' big corporate cronies who appreciate the cheap labor to pad their profits. And while some of these career politicians seem intent to stay in office as long as they are physically and mentally capable (and clearly long after, in some cases), most Americans look forward to retirement for years of hard work, eager to enjoy their time with their families using the money they earned.

I find it rather insulting to working class Americans seeing politicians riding the gravy train even after they're clearly incapable of responsibly or effectively representing citizens. They figure that as long as they're protected by the political establishment, they may as well enjoy the cushy gig at the expense of the American citizens and taxpayers.

The reality is that this practice won't stop until citizens stop it, and the way to stop it is by implementing term limits. George Washington set this precedent when he refused to serve for more than two terms as our nation's first President. After he had served faithfully, he went back to his farm on the Potomac. No one should be able to become wealthy and powerful by spending decades as a 'public servant.'

After industrious Americans have worked until their death to pay the bills, the government takes their pound of flesh in taxes, just as Grandma Otte learned those many years ago. This agenda to deny citizens the benefits of the retirement into which they paid for their working years just to fund an incompetent government machine has always struck me as rather repulsive. This likely stems from a powerful example that was set for me as a young man.

Back in the '80s, our "rural route" postal carrier in Seymour, Indiana was a rather extraordinary woman— John Mellencamp's mother, Marilyn. I was a huge fan of Mellencamp's music, having been born in the same small town, But I was perhaps a bigger fan of his mother, who I knew from when she delivered mail and packages to our home.

Usually, I wasn't around when she came by, but one day she brought a package when I happened to be there. I answered the door and we got to talking about her son's talent and success. I was incredibly impressed when she remarked that although her son was a successful rock star, she kept working her mail-carrier job. She explained that she was determined to qualify for her full postal service pension, as she had put in many years of hard work and paid into that retirement benefit program.

This is not only a Hoosier value but an American value— dedication to following through on commitments and achieving goals through hard work. Marilyn and so many others embody this value every day in this country, and that's why I am determined to fight for working people.

These are the people who are the backbone of this great nation, and they are at the mercy of those they assume represent their best interest, but who so often serve other agendas of power and control. This has never been more obvious to me than during these last few years.

The career-types in Washington have no clue about fiscal responsibility so they keep sticking the tab to the taxpayer and walking away, figuring someone else will deal with the problems they create.

It's especially repulsive when the 'conservative voices' in our own Republican Party thump their chests and talk a good game to placate voters, then contribute to the problem, knowing they're protected by the political establishment. They go on radio and TV telling the people how much they care about conservative values and the hardworking Americans, then they throw billions of our dollars in the trash by funding ridiculous activist agendas, failing government programs, or even other nations. After those billions are spent, they head home to relax for a few days to decide if they'll show up for the next vote.

I've spent decades working hard for everything I have and making sure Americans, and even people around the world, get fed. I'm a 6th generation Indiana farmer, and it's in my DNA to work hard and accomplish my goals. My goal now is to represent the best interest of the people in defense of an established political machine intent on maintaining their power.

I've already experienced first-hand their power as they have tried to crush me from day one of filing to run for the U.S. Senate. They are scared of me because they know they cannot control me. After being blessed by the freedoms and opportunities that are part of the American Dream, my campaign will be largely self-funded. I feel it is my turn to give back by entering public service to ensure this American Dream is available to future generations.

I don't need help from the political establishment and that terrifies them. I've never been more grateful for my ability to remain independent from those who wish to have control over me. A major reason I can remain independent is that I am donating the funds to my campaign, not loaning them, which is what most politicians do. Others loan the money to their own campaign and tell the voters they are self-funded, claiming that they aren't bought and paid for. But when they get to Washington, they solicit donations from PACs, mega-corporations, and other establishment entities to be able to pay themselves back for their loan to their own campaign. They end up bought and paid for after all, and the voters never even realize it.

My choice to donate my own money to my campaign means I will not be beholden to any special interest groups. I will be able to raise the curtain and shine a light on what is really going on in Washington without pressure from outside forces who feel I 'owe' them. Not only will I be free to do so, but I will have the gumption to actually do it.

I am determined to stand up for what is morally right and ultimately fight for the freedom, opportunity, and prosperity that the government is slowly stripping away. My boss will never be the powerful oligarchs of this nation like mega-corporations or controlling elites, who already own so much of our government. I won't be working for radical activists who seek to undermine fundamental American values and destroy the American Dream.

Voters hear this all the time from politicians who almost never follow through. But this promise is meaningful to me. I don't need this as a career or to get rich like so many in Washington do. I'm in this to do what is right, no matter the cost, a value ingrained in me since birth. I am so fearful of what is becoming of our nation at the hands of these captured career politicians. As a political outsider who has already fought for and won back the rights of 81% of Hoosiers to run for office, I will fight even harder once I'm in Washington as Indiana's next United States Senator.

My boss will be the people of Indiana—hardworking Hoosiers—who I will serve with the same dedication, tenacity, and work ethic I've lived by for these many decades.

Let us make America free again. Let us make America prosperous again. Let us make the work of all Americans valued again. Together, let us make America decent again.

PHOTOGRAPHS

David Rust (father of John Rust) in the original 500 hen chicken house, 1934.

Chester and David Rust in front of the original 500 hen chicken house, late 1930s.

Chester Rust in front of the second 500 hen chicken house,
early 1940s.

Lois Rust (baby), Everett & Lura Otte (mother and grandparents
of John Rust), 1934.

Otte Family Farm with Freeman Army Air Field in the distance.
The base was established in 1942 as a pilot training airfield and
adjoined the Otte Family farm near Seymour, Indiana, 1940s.

Grandpa Otte in the basement of their home showing a chicken
brooder, late 1930s. The chicks were kept in the basement for
health and warmth until old enough to live in the hen house.

Otte Family Farm.

1951 Oliver Row Crop 66 tractor being used to thrash wheat on the Otte Family farm. Grandpa Otte shown atop the wagon.

Otte family farm home.

Grandpa Otte atop a CO-OP brand tractor gathering straw
from the field, 1950s.

Walter Rust Family, 1953. Left to right: Waldron, David, Carol, Walter, Lillian, Vera, & Chester Rust.

"Dave's Produce" pickup truck at the Indianapolis Farmers Market (Indianapolis Municipal Market), early 1950s.

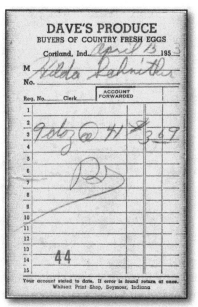

Dave's Produce payment slip for Hilda Schnitker showing
9 dozen eggs purchased at .41 cents a dozen. These eggs
would be candled (inspected & graded) then sold at
the Indianapolis Farmers Market.

Chester Rust, David Rust, & Bud Newark examining Dad's
Army service rifle, 1953. While Dad was in the service,
Chester Rust handled Dad's egg route in Indianapolis and helped
grow the business by adding more stores to the routes
until Dad returned home.

Marcus and Anthony Rust, first two children of David and Lois
Rust, playing in front of the first large "Rose Acre"
delivery truck, circa 1956.

Second "Rose Acres" truck, a 1956 Chevrolet. Used to pick up eggs
from Jackson County and neighboring farmers in the surrounding
areas for re-sale at the Indianapolis Farmers Market.

"Egg House," location of the first grading and cooler egg
storage facility, circa 1956.

Rose Acre Farms egg cartons, 1950s.

First chicken houses at the new Rose Acres—'Alabama,'
'Tennessee,' 'Kentucky,' 'Texas,' 'Siberia,' and 'Washington'—on
Baseline Road, 1957. Another large chicken house was added in
1961 which brought the total to 100,000 hens at this location.

Pentagon #1 (P1), first 'inline' cage-free egg farm where feeding,
egg production, grading, & cooling was all in one location!

GATHERING EGGS

Edna Lambert of Vallonia is pictured as she gathers eggs in a floor operation, the Pentagon 1 located north of Acme. Rose Acre Farms has two pentagons, with each having 7 wings with a capacity of 10,000 birds per wing, managed by one egg gatherer.

An egg gatherer pushing the cart while gathering eggs in a chicken house at Pentagon #1, 1960s. Used with permission, The Tribune.

John Rust with father, David, 1968. Note the 'Rust for Commissioner' lapel pin on Dad's jacket as he was running for political office when I was just a year old!

David Rust campaigning for Jackson County Commissioner, 1968.
Used with permission, The Tribune.

Ruth Ann (Rust) Hendrix going door to door
campaigning for Dad in 1968!

Rose Acre Farms Open House newspaper graphic.

Seymour Daily Tribune headline of the cornerstone being set for Egg Acres, 1969. Used with permission, The Tribune.

Eggs being cartoned after being washed and graded
at Egg Acres, 1970.

Egg Acres, first 'inline' caged egg laying complex built by our
family, November 1970.

Largest single order placed for laying cages

The biggest single order for laying cages was placed recently by Dave Rust, Rose Acre Farms, Seymour, Ind.

The order involved cages for 1,200,000 layers which will be used in Rust's new production complex, known as Jenn-Acres, located on U.S. 50 east of North Vernon, Ind.

A 1970s article highlighting how the order for equipment to build Jen Acres near North Vernon, Indiana, was the largest of its kind in United States history. Used with permission, The Tribune.

Ruth Ann (Rust) Hendrix & John Rust with the very first Rose Acres hatched chick near Acme, Indiana.

Walter & Lillian Rust with grandkids (John Rust on Grandpa Rust's lap). From left: Leah Rust, Danny Hoevener, James Rust, Grandpa, Karen Rust, John Rust, Gloria Hoevener, Mary Kay Kastner, Grandma Rust holding Robert Rust, Ruth Ann Rust, Rick Kastner, Annette Hoevener, Anthony Rust, & Marcus Rust.

Rust family on the front porch of our home next to Jen Acres—Anthony, James, Karen, Ruth Ann, Robert, Marcus, & John, 1971.

John Rust growing up as a typical farm kid.

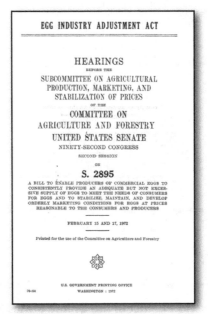

EGG INDUSTRY ADJUSTMENT ACT

HEARINGS
BEFORE THE
SUBCOMMITTEE ON AGRICULTURAL
PRODUCTION, MARKETING, AND
STABILIZATION OF PRICES
OF THE
COMMITTEE ON
AGRICULTURE AND FORESTRY
UNITED STATES SENATE
NINETY-SECOND CONGRESS
SECOND SESSION
ON

S. 2895

A BILL TO ENABLE PRODUCERS OF COMMERCIAL EGGS TO
CONSISTENTLY PROVIDE AN ADEQUATE BUT NOT EXCES-
SIVE SUPPLY OF EGGS TO MEET THE NEEDS OF CONSUMERS
FOR EGGS AND TO STABILIZE, MAINTAIN, AND DEVELOP
ORDERLY MARKETING CONDITIONS FOR EGGS AT PRICES
REASONABLE TO THE CONSUMERS AND PRODUCERS

FEBRUARY 15 AND 17, 1972

Printed for the use of the Committee on Agriculture and Forestry

U.S. GOVERNMENT PRINTING OFFICE
WASHINGTON : 1972

Egg Industry Adjustment Act. This act would have meant the end of the free market for United States egg production. David Rust & family fought hard against this for the following two decades to make sure marketing orders that artificially raised egg prices would not be implemented in the United States.

Mr. FOSTER. Well, it is a long-range program. I am not up here to tell them what to do, but for goodness sake do something, so I can go home and tell the bankers that they are doing something.

Senator JORDAN. We appreciate your being here. And we will try to help you as best we can.

Mr. FOSTER. I would like to ask one question.

Senator JORDAN. Yes, indeed

Mr. FOSTER. We have a tobacco program in Georgia. It doesn't cost the Government much money. We are not asking for a floor plan on these eggs. We went to this meeting, we all went down there, chickenmen—you know how they are. I cut off two houses.

We need somebody to tell us what we have got to do. If our parents didn't tell us we would have been in an awful mess. We just want somebody to help us.

Senator JORDAN. Fine. Thank you very much.

Mr. Rust, Rose Acre Farms, Seymour, Ind.

Proceed as you like, sir.

STATEMENT OF DAVID W. RUST, ROSE ACRE FARMS, SEYMOUR, IND.

Mr. RUST. My name is David W. Rust, I was born and raised on a hill farm in southern Indiana.

My wife, seven children and I own an egg production farm which consists of a breeder flock, hatchery, pullet growing houses, layer facilities, egg processing, a feed mill, and egg routes to city and country stores in our immediate area.

We are opposed to industry and governmental controls in agricultural food production.

Because approximately 10,000 people per day are dying from starvation and malnutrition.

Because if we are to continue our Christian leadership in food production in a starving world we must remain free. If any person or group of persons is capable of producing more efficiently than we, this inherent right must be maintained.

Because industry restriction and government intervention in other farming areas have hindered progress.

Because overproduction causes lower prices and increases consumption and this in turn causes lower production and higher prices, which in turn cause overexpansion and a repeated cycle. These two extremes cause the very beneficial effects of increased efficiency, more modern facilities, lower costs to the consumers and increased consumption.

Because when controls are first inaugurated the people appointed are usually well qualified, but succeeding appointments invariably cater to interests not directly affiliated with consumer and agricultural interests. They are not usually knowledgeable and current with the latest industry trends and therefore the poultry industry and society as a whole must suffer.

Because approximately 70 people have died from starvation and malnutrition in the past 10 minutes. To help guarantee the survival of our country—for our children—as a free Nation—food production must remain free.

(Attachments to the statement follow:)

Statement of David W. Rust in the United States Senate hearing on consideration of marketing orders in the United States.

Two Different Views

David Rust, Seymour, Ind., center, offers his views to Fred Adams of Edwards, Miss., right, as Bev Yeiser, Winchester, Ky., looks on. Scene was a break in the hearings on the Egg Industry Adjustment Act. Rust testified in opposition to the bill. Adams is president of United Egg Producers which is supporting the measure.

Newspaper article. Used with permission, The Tribune.

John Rust with his carved pumpkin, Halloween 1974.

John Rust, July 4, 1976.

Bob Myers (Jackson County FFA Chairman), John Rust,
& David Rust, Labor Day 1976.

Rust family, including John, at a ceremony honoring our nation's birth by raising a flag on the new 100-foot-tall flagpole at Jen Acres, Fall 1976. Similar flagpoles are located at nearly all our Indiana farms.

100-foot-tall flagpole at Rose Acre Farms headquarters near Seymour, Indiana. During the bicentennial year of 1976, our family proudly celebrated our nation's 200th birthday by erecting giant flagpoles at our Jen Acre and Rose Acre facilities.

John and Robert Rust showing off the latest in farm boy fashion.

"Farming is Everybody's Bread and Butter." Karen and John Rust boating down the Amazon River to tour a farm, 1977.

A summertime look inside one of the chicken houses at Pentagon #2 showing roughly 1/2 the chickens in that hen house, the eggs from which would all be gathered by one person!

Lura Otte, right, keeps up with changes in estate tax laws and alters her estate plan accordingly. "These days a widow needs all the help she can get," she tells the author, Laura Lane, left. Mrs. Otte especially values the continuing support of two sons and three daughters, all in farming. The youngest son, unmarried, lives in the family home with her. Mrs. Otte remains a record-keeper and keen analyst of commodity market trends.

Reporter Laura Lane with Grandma Otte at the Otte Farm just west of Seymour, Indiana, shortly after Grandma Otte won her court case in a victory for farm families across the United States, August 1979. Used with permission, The Farm Journal Magazine.

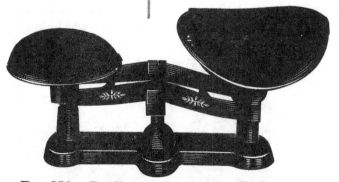

Advertisement by Rose Acre Farms during the building of Cort Acres highlighting the need for the rights of farmers to be able to use their land to help feed America.

Took too long

We are glad that a stay order halting work on Dave Rust's Sand Acre chicken operation in neighboring Jackson county has been lifted and, at long last, work can be resumed on completing this project.

To show you how things can crawl along, these Sand Acre facilities were destroyed in the 1974 tornado. Most of the time since then, Rust has been battling to rebuild them. He thought that he had every obstacle out of the way last year, and finally started work on the project, including hatching the baby chickens that he planned to house in the Sand Acre facility. But along came this suit, and things ground to a halt again.

Wisely, we think, the judge in this case has said in effect, that while an "i" might not have been dotted nor a "t" crossed the way it should technically have been in some of the actions of the governing bodies who okayed Rust's plan to rebuild these were only "irregularities" and not "illegalities."

It doesn't seem right to us that the delay should have been the long one it was. There ought to be a way, which would give full protection to people and needed environmental controls, where the "yea" or the "nay" comes much faster than it did in this matter.

Reprinted From North Vernon Plain Dealer

Reprinted from the North Vernon Plain Dealer newspaper in the Seymour Daily Tribune, May 4, 1978. Used with permission, The Tribune.

Placard for Freedom of Speech and Property Rights displayed by many Jackson County businesses and homes in support of the building of Cort Acres, late 1970s.

When built, Cort Acres was the largest egg farm in the world. Over 40 years later, it continues to produce over 2,000,000 eggs a day, helping feed people throughout the world.

Rose Acre Farms and Jackson County Future Farmers of America
take a joint trip to our nation's capital, March 29, 1979.
In the front row without hats are Linda Myers & John Rust.
Linda works as a leader in FFA today, continuing the efforts
of her father, Bob Myers.

John Rust with a Remington 20 gauge shot gun for Christmas!

Lois, John, & David Rust at the Rose Acre Farms Christmas Party & Awards banquet, 1982.

Confirmation class photo at St. Paul Lutheran Church (Borchers). Front row from left: Julie Otte (partly obscured), Kim Otte, Jean Wanamaker, Don Rotert, Donna Wanamaker, Michelle Waskcom, Marie Claycamp. Back row: John Rust, Tony Reichenba, Michael Schafstall, Kevin Kruse.

DAUGHTER of Egg Acres owner David Rust, Karen Rust of the Cortland area at right waits for firefighters to give the okay to open doors in six chicken houses not on fire to prevent suffocation of the 200,000 laying hens housed there. With her are employees of the firm. The go-ahead was given moments later.

During emergencies at a farm, it is always "all hands on deck."
Karen Rust (left) getting ready to enter chicken houses to open the
"knock out doors" so that the hens could safely breath fresh air.
Used with permission, The Tribune.

John and Lois Rust at a Saturday Night Meeting at the Ponderosa
Steak House in Seymour, Indiana, circa 1983. This was a route
sales meeting and the numbers on the boards behind us were the
miles per gallon by truck listed individually for the entire Rose Acre
Fleet. Efficiency in every aspect was always monitored
by everyone at Rose Acre Farms.

John Rust at a bulldozer building a dam to house a good-sized reservoir of water.

Animal Liberation Front attacks, July 2, 2000. The ALF Terrorist group burned the feed truck at our Jen Acre farm causing over $100,000 in damage. This attack was the first volley in a long war with eco-terrorists intent on depriving Americans of wholesome, inexpensive eggs.

Graffiti painted on the side of the feed mill at Jen Acres—
"Polluter, Animal Exploiter! Your turn to Pay! ALF."

A letter by my father lamenting the jury verdict that found
our family guilty of selling eggs too cheaply. Rose Acre Farms
has always been proud of the fact that we have helped make
eggs one of the greatest food bargains you can find at the grocery
store. The free enterprise system and free markets make eggs
an incredible food value.

John Rust at the farm where he spent many days (and nights) keeping the hens watered and eggs gathered during the blizzards of 1978!

Judge sides with Seymour egg firm in decade-old case

By Jeff Swiatek

jeff.swiatek@indystar.com

The "good egg people" have bested Uncle Sam.

A U.S. Court of Federal Claims judge in Washington, D.C., has ordered the federal government to pay $6.1 million plus 12 years' interest to Rose Acre Farms.

The order, released by the court this week, comes in the Indiana egg giant's long-running lawsuit against the federal government over salmonella regulations Rose Acre considered unfair.

In often-blunt language, Judge Bohdan A. Futey said the government must compensate Rose Acre for monetary losses due to "misguided" regulations.

"The court concludes the (salmonella) regulations were misguided because they relied on ineffective testing methods," the judge said in the 32-page ruling that followed a bench trial last spring. "It is true that the public has a strong interest in eating safe food, however the regulations at issue went too far."

The regulations, passed in 1990, threatened to put Seymour-based Rose Acre out of business, according to testimony in the case. Rose Acre, which has used the advertising jingle "the good egg people," ranks as one of the nation's largest egg producers.

Executives at the family-owned business "decided to continue on and fight this to survive, and that's exactly what they did," said Robert R. Clark, an Indianapolis attorney with the firm of Sommer Barnard Ackerson, which represented Rose Acre in the case.

Clark said his firm will petition the court separately to order the government to also pay Rose Acre's legal fees, which top $1 million.

Responding to outbreaks of salmonella poisoning, the U.S. Department of Agriculture put in place emergency regulations at egg farms to crack down on cases of poisoning from the bacteria, which is found in the intestinal tracts of birds and animals.

Rose Acre became a focus of regulatory action after three outbreaks of salmonella poisoning in 1990 in Kentucky, Illinois and Tennessee were traced to suspect eggs from three of its farms in Indiana. The worst outbreak caused 400 people to become ill after eating bread pudding at a True Value Hardware convention in Chicago.

Citing the new regulations, government regulators refused to allow Rose Acre to sell eggs in the shell from the three egg farms and mandated expensive wet-cleaning of the hen houses that damaged their electrical wiring. Rose Acre was forced to sell at a loss 700 million eggs that were diverted into low-priced markets for eggs that are broken and pasteurized because they typically don't meet the standards for retail eggs sold in the shell.

The judge said the government never tested any Rose Acre eggs for salmonella during or after the poisoning incidents. As such, it couldn't be sure if bacteria were in the eggs when shipped or introduced later due to improper handling or food preparation, or whether later shipments of eggs contained salmonella.

"In light of the fact that defendant never tested plaintiff's eggs, the court does not believe defendant has established that plaintiff had a (salmonella) problem," the judge said.

Clark said the 1990 USDA egg regulations remain on the books but haven't been enforced since the mid-1990s.

A spokesman at the Department of Justice, which defended the government in the case, said the ruling is under review and it's not known if an appeal will be filed.

The case landed in the claims court in 1992 after the 7th Circuit Court of Appeals in Chicago suggested it be litigated there.

■ Call Jeff Swiatek at 1-317-444-6483.

Indianapolis Star 9-5-02.

Indianapolis Star, September 5, 2002.

Chickens at Rose Acre Farms, September 1997.

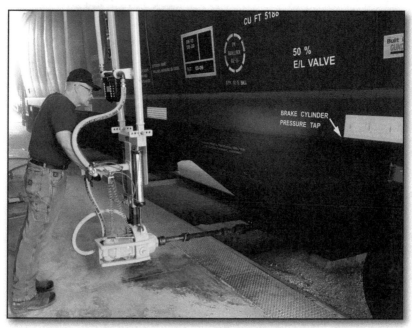

John Rust unloading grain at the Lone Cactus Egg Farm.

John Rust engineering empty grain cars after being unloaded at the farm.

John & Lois Rust at the Lone Cactus Egg Farm, 2021

Karen, Robert, & John Rust at the EggLife Foods grand opening in Walcott, Indiana, 2019. In addition to being Chairman of the Board of Rose Acre Farms, John was Chairman of the Board of EggLife Foods until running for the United States Senate.
EggLife Foods produces low carb wraps made from egg whites, which are available nationwide as a low carb alternative to wraps made from flour.

John Rust with a baby chick at a new cage-free Rose Acre hen house.

Marcus Rust, Shirley Allen, & John Rust at the Baur House in Winterset, Iowa, sight of the first Rose Acre egg farm in Iowa.

The extended Rust family for Christmas at the home of Luiz & John!

John Rust with Brian Teulker at the Cort Acre 'can-off' line where pasteurized liquid egg product is cartoned for retail sale.

Back row: Marcus Rust, Elias Hendrix, Bryce McCory, Karen Rust, John Rust, Robert Rust, Paul Rust, Christopher Rust, and James Rust. Front row: Ruth Ann Hendrix, Lois Rust, & Moriah Hendrix.

John Rust with Luiz's nephews Gustavo & Joao, visiting from Brazil and seeing snow for the first time!

John Rust with Kim Sanchez at Cort Acres.

John Rust with Greg Davis at Cort Acres.

Gary Bradley & John Rust. In background is the Oliver 66 Tractor purchased by John's Grandma Otte for use on the farm. The receipt for that tractor helped set a nationwide legal precedent to save farm wives from having to pay estate tax at the time of their partner's death.

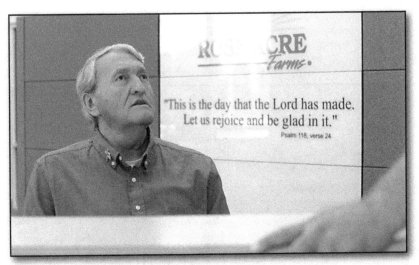

Gary Bradley at the Rose Acre 'front desk.'

John Rust with Linda Myers at the 2nd Annual Jackson County FFA
Scholarship fundraising dinner!

John Rust at County Line Egg Farm near Frankfort, Indiana, 2023.

Christmas at the farm! Chickens don't take holidays off, so we don't either! Lois & John Rust with the crew of the farm working hard to get the day's production out so everyone could return home to be with their families!

Tony Wesner, Robert Rust, Bruce Williams, John Rust, & Marcus Rust at the 2023 Rose Acre Farms Southern Indiana awards dinner, recognizing Bruce for 40 years of service!

John Rust with Steve Starr.

John Rust driving his 1972 Ford F100 pickup!

John Rust at the organ at St. Paul Lutheran Church. He is a
substitute organist for services when Olga Otte is unavailable.

John Rust with nephew Mark & niece Julia at the Rust for U.S. Senate Campaign office!

Campaign Office Opening.

Campaign Office Opening.

Campaign Office Opening.

Campaign Office Opening.

John Rust at the Indiana boyhood home of Abraham Lincoln, who famously said, "Elections belong to the people. It's their decision."

John Rust with Gayle Skaggs.

**John Rust out on the campaign trail being interviewed by
21 Alive in Fort Wayne.**

**John Rust with Ann Rosebery, Julie Schroder,
& Connie Newkirk Johnson.**

John Rust with Florence Otte.

John Rust with Craig Zody.

John Rust with Dalton Demny at Eagle Rail Car Services in
Washington, Indiana.

John Rust on the campaign trail.

John Rust with Duane McClintock.

John and Luiz at McDonalds in Huntington, Indiana.

John Rust with Ram Jackson.

John Rust with Michelle Harter & her father, Michael Maher, on
the date of my court hearing which ultimately gave voice to the
81% of Hoosiers who had previously been banned from running
for political office! John is wearing a vintage 1976 American flag tie
celebrating our nations independence.

179

John Rust with Beckie Madigan.

John Rust with Rick Paris & Carter.

John Rust with the Coopers in Vernon, Indiana.

John Rust speaking at an event in Shelbyville, Indiana.

Maxi is for Rust!!!!!!

ABOUT THE AUTHOR

JOHN RUST GREW UP alongside the chickens on his family's farms. What started as nothing more than a dream and a pickup truck has become one of the country's leading producers of a healthy and affordable source of nutrition—eggs. He spent decades working on the farms, which shaped him into a man who values hard work, freedom, and the American Dream. After seeing that dream threatened by corruption and authoritarianism, he shifted his focus from eggs to America. Now, John is using his farmer's work ethic to fight for the principles and values that made this country one where a smalltown farmer can grow a nationwide business or represent his fellow Americans in the U.S. Senate!

Printed in the USA
CPSIA information can be obtained
at www.ICGtesting.com
LVHW010302270424
778357LV00004B/6/J